Beaded Lace Knitting

Beaded Lace Knitting

Anniken Allis

STACKPOLE
BOOKS

Published by
STACKPOLE BOOKS
5067 Ritter Road
Mechanicsburg, PA 17055
www.stackpolebooks.com

Printed in the United States of America

10 9 8 7 6 5 4 3 2 1

First edition

Cover design by Caroline M. Stover
Project photography by Burcu Avsar
How-to photography by Rob Frost

Library of Congress Cataloging-in-Publication Data

Allis, Anniken.
  Beaded lace knitting : techniques and 24 beaded lace designs
for shawls, scarves & more / Anniken Allis. — First edition.
    pages cm
  ISBN 978-0-8117-1457-0
1. Bead crochet. 2. Knitted lace—Patterns. 3. Dress accessories. I. Title.
  TT861.3.A45 2015
  746.43—dc23
                        2015004659

Contents

Acknowledgments

Growing up in Norway, I learned to knit at a very young age. After returning to knitting after a break of a few years, I discovered lace knitting. I was given Jane Sowerby's book *Victorian Lace Today* as a Christmas present by my in-laws and through Jane's book I fell in love with lace knitting.

A few years later I learned how to add beads using a crochet hook and I'm now hooked on beautiful beaded lace patterns. They can be easy to knit or challenging but they're always beautiful.

I'd like to thank my Mum for teaching me to knit and for helping me develop my knitting skills throughout my childhood and teenage years. Thank you to my editor, Pam Hoenig, and the team at Stackpole Books for giving me this opportunity to write my dream book. Thank you to my husband, Simon, and my daughters, Vanessa and Emily, for putting up with me while I wrote this book. There were stressful times and times when our house was covered in yarns and lace shawls.

A lot of knitting has gone into producing this book and I couldn't have done it without my wonderful team of sample knitters. Thank you to Anita Cross, Leni McCormick, Judy Wilmot, Liz Agnew, Frances Jago, Jen Snow, Michelle Lincoln, Debs Legge, and Nicky Sutton for all their hard work and amazing knitting skills. Thank you also to all the yarn companies who provided the beautiful yarns used in this book; their yarns are listed in each pattern. The choice of yarns these days is amazing and I love working with beautiful yarns.

I'd also like to thank the knitters who support my work. The feedback I get from you encourages me to keep designing. I hope you enjoy this book and please do get in touch. I love seeing what you knit from my patterns. You can find me via my website, yarnaddict.co.uk, or through social media. I'm YarnAddictAnni on Ravelry, Twitter, Instagram, and Pinterest and my Facebook page is www.facebook.com/yarnaddictbyannikenallis.—Anniken

Introduction

I've been knitting for as long as I can remember and the more I learn about knitting, the more I realize there is to learn. In my knitting "career" I have experimented with a variety of techniques. Growing up in Norway, I learned traditional Norwegian stranded colorwork at an early age. When I returned to knitting as an adult, I taught myself, with the help of books and the Internet, to knit cables and lace. And although I enjoy all these techniques, lace knitting is the technique that inspires me the most.

My first design was published in 2007, a pair of socks with a lacy heart motif. I then went on to design more socks, as well as shawls, mittens, other accessories, and garments. I use a variety of techniques in my designs but the one I keep coming back to is lace knitting. It never gets boring.

Lace knitting can be very simple or very complicated. You can knit lace in very, very fine yarn or in bulky yarn. And it is this variety that captivates me. You can use lace knitting for a delicate shawl or a chunky hat. There are endless design possibilities.

In this book I decided to combine lace and beads in heirloom quality designs. The beads add a bit of bling and luxury to lace patterns. However, if beads aren't your thing, these lace designs are beautiful without them, too.

Whether you've never knitted lace before or consider yourself an expert lace knitter, you will find patterns in this book suitable for you. If you find it difficult to learn the techniques from the photos and instructions, search online for video tutorials. Keep practicing! It doesn't matter if you make a mistake. You can rip out your knitting and use the yarn again. Just think of it as better value for the money.

These days we have more choice in yarn than ever before. We can order yarn from almost anywhere in the world. We can choose from cheap man-made fibers to the finest animal fibers (ever heard of qiviut? It's the champagne of yarn). Yarn comes in all price ranges. I like knitting with natural fibers and I admit to being a yarn snob. My preference is for good quality natural fibers. I have tried in this book to use yarn across a range of prices. If the yarn suggested in a pattern is too expensive for you, there will be cheaper alternatives. If a yarn isn't available where you live, don't be afraid of choosing something different. Read the section on substituting yarn.

Knitting should be fun! Yes, it can be stressful, challenging, and frustrating at times but overall it should be fun. So try to enjoy your knitting. Don't give up! Keep practicing! If a pattern is a bit too challenging, choose an easier one and come back to the challenging one when you have more experience.

I hope you enjoy this book as much as I've enjoyed creating it. Happy knitting!

Lace and Beading Techniques

Lace knitting looks very complex but is really just a combination of increases and decreases. Learn a few basic techniques, choose a beautiful yarn, add some beads, and you can create stunning heirloom pieces that will impress knitters and non-knitters alike.

It is important in lace knitting to use the correct decreases as these shape the fabric and, together with yarn overs, create the lace pattern.

Remember, there is a huge amount of information available online for knitters. If you're unsure of a technique that is not covered here, do an online search and you will probably find many written, photographic, and video tutorials. Some tutorials are of better quality than others, so check a few out before proceeding. You can also check out my website, www.yarnaddict.co.uk, and click on Tutorials.

Lace Stitches

Some stitches used in lace knitting are worked slightly differently for English-style and continental-style knitters; where necessary, I have shown both styles. I am a continental knitter, so most of the technique photos are shown knitting/holding the yarn continental style.

In lace patterns every yarn over is usually balanced out by a decrease. The decreases can be placed right next to the yarn over, several stitches away, or on a different row. Pattern repeats will start and end on the same stitch count, unless you are increasing. If there are more yarn overs than decreases, then you will be increasing the stitch count. If there are more decreases than yarn overs, then you will be decreasing the stitch count.

Yarn Overs

Yarn overs create the holes in lace knitting. You are increasing a stitch by taking the yarn over the right needle to create a new stitch. On the next row this stitch is either purled or knitted.

English-Style Knitters

Yarn over between two knit stitches: Take your yarn to the front between the needles, hold it as you would if you were about to purl the next stitch. You are now ready to knit the next stitch and you will have created a loop over your right needle.

Yarn over after a knit stitch and before a purl stitch: Take the yarn to the front between the needles, over the right needle to the back, and between the two needles to the front again. You will have wrapped the yarn completely around the right needle and will be ready to purl the next stitch.

Yarn over between two purl stitches: As you have just worked a purl stitch, the working yarn will be at the front. Take the yarn over the right needle to the back and then between the two needles to the front, ready to purl the next stitch.

Yarn over after a purl stitch and before a knit stitch: As you have just worked a purl stitch, the working yarn will be at the front. Leave the yarn at the front, then you will be ready to knit the next stitch.

Continental-Style Knitters

Yarn over between two knit stitches: Take the yarn between the needles to the front, then over the right needle to the back, ready to knit the next stitch.

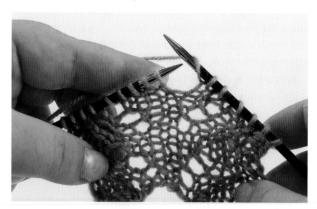

If you purl with the yarn at the back (i.e., Norwegian purl), a yarn over between a knit and a purl stitch or between two purl stitches is worked in the same way as between two knit stitches. You take the yarn between the needles to the front, then over the right needle to the back. You have now created the yarn over. Move your needle and yarn into the right position to purl the next stitch.

If you purl with the yarn at the front (i.e., regular continental purl), take the yarn between the needles to the front, then over the right needle, then take the yarn to the front so you are ready to purl the next stitch.

Decreases

In lace knitting, decreases help to shape the lace pattern and it's important to work the correct directional decreases (right-slanting or left-slanting); otherwise, it may affect the final look of your lace pattern. In garter stitch, it's less important to work directional decreases as it won't affect the final look.

Knit 2 (or 3) stitches together (k2tog/k3tog): This is a right-slanting decrease that will decrease the stitch count by 1 or 2 stitches. Insert the right needle into the next 2 or 3 stitches and knit them together to make 1 stitch.

Purl 2 (or 3) stitches together (p2tog/p3tog): As with k2tog/k3tog, this decreases the stitch count by 1 or 2 stitches with a decrease that leans to the right when seen from the knit side of the fabric. Insert the right needle purl-wise into the next 2 or 3 stitches and purl them together to make 1 stitch.

Slip, slip, (slip), knit (ssk/sssk): This decreases 1 or 2 stitches, producing a left-slanting stitch. As shown right, slip the first stitch knitwise, slip the next stitch knitwise (if working a sssk, slip a third stitch knitwise), insert the left needle tip into the front of these 2 or 3 stitches, and knit together. You are twisting the stitches and knitting them together through the back loops.

1. Slip 1 stitch knitwise.

2. Slip the next stitch knitwise.

3. Insert the left needle into the front of both stitches and knit together.

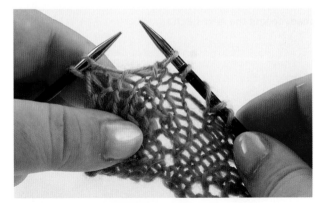

4. The ssk after it's been worked.

Slip, slip, (slip), purl (ssp/sssp): This is the purl version of the ssk/sssk and decreases 1 or 2 stitches with a decrease that leans to the left when seen from the knit side. Slip 1 stitch knitwise, slip the next stitch knitwise (if working a sssp, slip a third stitch knitwise), place these stitches back on the left needle, and purl through the back loops.

Final stage (p2tog tbl) of ssp with yarn held English style.

Sl1, k2tog, psso: This is a double decrease that reduces 3 stitches to 1 stitch. Slip 1 stitch knitwise, knit 2 stitches together, pass slipped stitch over the k2tog stitch.

1. Slip 1 stitch knitwise.

2. Knit 2 stitches together.

3. Pass slipped stitch over to complete the sl1, k2tog, psso.

Sl2, k1, p2 sso: This is another double decrease that reduces 3 stitches to 1 stitch. Slip 2 stitches (slip both together) knitwise, knit 1, and pass the 2 slipped stitches over the knit stitch.

Making Lace Knitting Easier

Probably the biggest challenge in lace knitting is keeping track of where you are. Here are some ways to help.

Stitch Markers

Stitch markers are great tools for keeping track of where you are in your pattern. I recommend using smooth ring markers for lace knitting. Handmade or fancy stitch markers can get tangled up in your delicate yarn. A length of waste yarn can also be used. Place a stitch marker between each pattern repeat or to mark off edgings or center stitches and to help with shaping. Most stitch markers sit on the needle between stitches, but locking stitch markers, which attach directly to the fabric, are also available.

When a stitch marker is placed next to a yarn over, it can sometimes slip through to the other side of the yarn over and end up in the wrong place. Watch out for this, especially when using stitch markers to mark a "center spine" stitch (as in a triangular top-down shawl). In cases like this, it may be better to use a locking stitch marker and attach it to the center spine stitch.

This is how stitch markers can make tracking your knitting so much easier. Let's say your pattern repeat is 10 stitches. If you finish a row and only have 99 stitches when you should have 100 stitches, trying to find the mistake can be difficult. If you have placed a stitch marker between each pattern repeat (every 10 stitches), count the stitches between each marker and you'll easily find the pattern repeat with only 9 stitches. Then you can go through those stitches to find your error.

Stitch markers can also be used to mark the yarn-over increases along the spine in a triangular shawl, to remind you when to work the yarn-over increases.

Finally, stitch markers can be used to keep track of shaping within a lace pattern. Garment patterns will quite often tell you to shape (increase or decrease) while keeping the stitch pattern correct. It is critical to remember that each yarn over must have a corresponding decrease; otherwise, you will be increasing the stitch count. When working various types of shaping, it's important to make sure you know which yarn overs and decreases "belong together" (i.e., balance each other out).

Begin by identifying the first and last pattern repeat. Depending on how big the pattern repeat is and how the yarn overs and decreases in the pattern repeat are organized, you may be able to divide the pattern repeat in half.

Decreasing: Place a marker after the first pattern repeat and before the last pattern repeat of the row. These stitches will now be worked plain with no lace patterning. Continue to work in the stitch pattern between the markers. Once you've decreased enough stitches to reach the markers, move the markers another repeat in and work these stitches plain from now on.

Increasing: Again, use stitch markers to separate the increased stitches from the pattern repeat. Once you have enough stitches increased to work a full or partial pattern repeat, incorporate the lace pattern into your increased section.

Reading Your Knitting

I strongly recommend that you look at your knitting as you work the various decreases and yarn overs and that you learn to visually distinguish the different decreases. This will make it so much easier for you to identify and correct errors. The only way to learn to "read" your knitting is to pay attention to what is coming off your needles as you work various stitches.

Using a Lifeline

A lifeline is a piece of waste yarn inserted through the stitches. You carry on knitting and if you make a mistake later on, you can rip back the knitting to the lifeline and your stitches will be sitting on the waste yarn, ready to slip back onto your needles. No worries about dropping stitches and stitches unraveling too far down. Make sure that your knitting is correct before inserting the lifeline. You can put in a lifeline after each pattern repeat, before

commencing shaping, or when you get to a difficult bit of the pattern that you are unsure about.

To insert a lifeline, take a piece of smooth yarn slightly thinner or the same thickness as your working yarn (for lace weight yarn, I recommend using a smooth fingering weight yarn). Using a blunt tapestry needle, thread the yarn through all your stitches while leaving them on the needle. This is easier if you use a circular needle and push all the stitches onto the cable, as you will have more space to thread the tapestry needle through.

Thread the waste yarn through all the stitches on your needle.

A lifeline has been inserted.

Secure the waste yarn by tying ends together. Continue knitting.

If you make a mistake and need to unravel several rows, you can take your needles out and unravel down to the lifeline; your stitches will be held safely on the waste yarn and you can place them back on your needle and continue knitting.

This shows several rows worked after a lifeline (the pink yarn is the lifeline).

If your knitting is correct, remove the lifeline and reinsert it. Lifelines can be inserted at the end of each pattern repeat or every 10 or 20 rows, for example. It can also be useful to insert a lifeline if you're starting another section of the pattern or starting a shaping section.

Casting On

All cast-ons are not created equal. When it matters, I may call for a particular type of cast-on in a pattern; otherwise, you can choose the cast-on that suits you.

Knitted Cast-On

Make a slip knot and place it on your needle. Hold the needle in your left hand, insert your right needle into the stitch created by the slip knot, and knit up a stitch as normal but leave the original loop on your left needle and place your new stitch on your left needle. You will now have 2 stitches. Continue until you have the correct number of stitches.

Cable Cast-On

This is very similar to the knitted cast-on but looks better. Make a slip knot and place it on your needle. Hold the needle in your left hand, insert the right needle into the stitch created by the slip knot, and knit up a stitch as normal. Leave the original stitch on the left needle and place the new stitch on the left needle. You now have 2 stitches. *Next, insert your needle between the first and second stitches on the left needle, knit up a new stitch as normal, and place it on the left needle. You now have 3 stitches. Continue (repeating from *) until you have the correct number of stitches.

Provisional Cast-Ons

A provisional cast-on is an open cast-on which will leave a row of live stitches that you can later pick up and knit into or knit in the other direction. There are several different provisional cast-ons, the provisional crochet cast-on probably being the most common. Personally, I prefer the invisible cast-on. I'll show you both of these methods but you can find demo videos and instructions for several others on various websites.

Provisional Crochet Cast-On

Using a piece of waste yarn and a crochet hook of similar size to your knitting needles and working yarn (if you are using a lace weight yarn, use a waste yarn that is a bit thicker), crochet a chain a few stitches longer than the number of stitches you want to cast on.

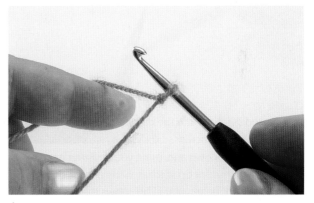

1. With your waste yarn, start with a slip knot on your crochet hook and hold the hook in your right hand.

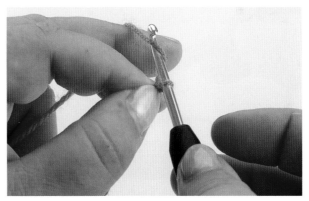

2. Hold the yarn in your left hand and wrap the yarn over the hook.

(continued)

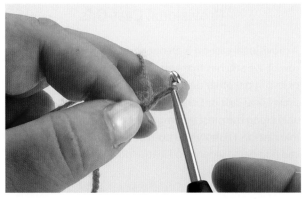

3. Pull the yarn through the stitch on the hook. This creates one chain. Repeat last 2 steps until the chain is as long as you need.

6. Insert the needle into the next bump.

4. Turn the chain over and, using your knitting needle and working yarn, pick up stitches in the bumps on the back of the crochet chain. This shows the bumps on the back of the crochet chain.

7. Two stitches picked up in the crochet chain.

5. One stitch picked up into a bump on the back of the crochet chain.

8. A row of stitches picked up in the crochet chain. You are now ready to start your knitting.

Working Into the Provisional Cast-On

When you want to undo your provisional cast-on, simply unzip the crochet chain and place the live stitches on a knitting needle. You need to unzip the crochet chain from the end you finished crocheting, so it's a good idea to leave a loop, several knots, or something similar to make sure you unzip from the right end.

1. Unzip the first stitch and place it on a knitting needle.

2. Continue to unzip the stitches.

3. Several stitches that have been unzipped and placed on a knitting needle. Once all the stitches are on the needle, you will have one stitch less than the number you cast on.

4. After the crochet chain has been unzipped and removed.

Invisible Cast-On

You need one knitting needle, your working yarn, and some waste yarn for this cast-on. Choose a waste yarn that's a similar thickness or slightly thicker than your working yarn. The waste yarn should be smooth and in a different color than your working yarn. In the photos, the pink yarn is the waste yarn and the blue is the working yarn.

Always hold your right index finger on top of the last loop cast on the needle, to keep it from slipping off the needle.

If you are casting on a large number of stitches, the loops can start twisting and sliding around the needle and you may lose a few stitches, so it may be best to choose another provisional cast-on. This method is suitable for the designs in this book that require a provisional cast-on. If you're unsure if you've counted correctly, cast on a few extra stitches. Only knit the number of stitches required for the pattern and unravel the rest.

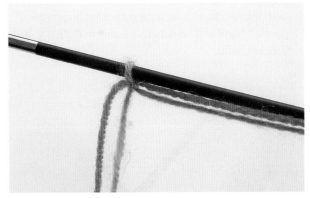

1. Tie a slip knot in your working yarn, put it on your knitting needle, and insert the end of the waste yarn through the slip knot.

2. Hold the two yarn ends and your knitting needle in your right hand. Put your right index finger on the slip knot to keep it secure.

(continued)

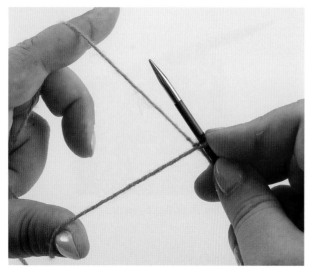

3. Take the waste yarn over your left thumb and the working yarn over your left index finger.

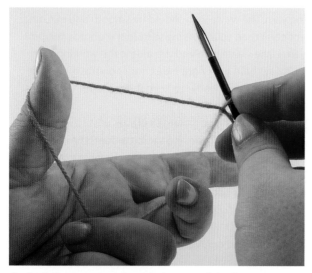

4. Grab the two strands with the rest of the fingers on your left hand and hold them securely in the palm of your left hand.

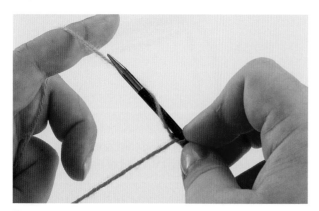

5. Take your needle outside and under the working yarn.

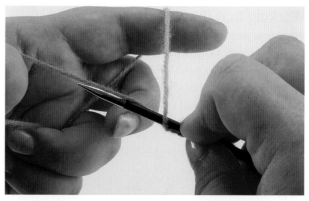

6. *Take the needle toward you and dip it under the waste yarn away from you.

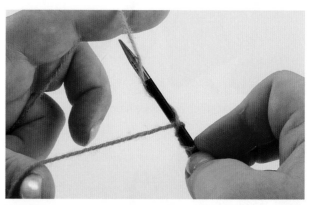

7. Take the needle outside and under the working yarn.

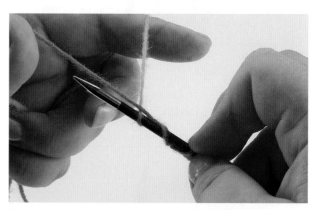

8. Continue under the waste yarn toward you.

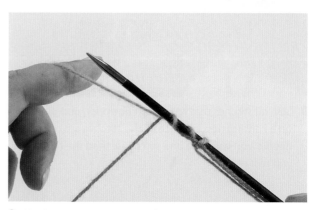

9. You've now cast on 2 stitches. Don't count the slip knot.

Continue until you've cast on the correct number of stitches. This method creates an even number of stitches. If you need an odd number of stitches, start from * to cast on a single stitch, then continue to cast on in pairs of two as before.

See how the waste yarn crosses in front of the working yarn in the photo below? It's important that the waste yarn crosses in front of the working yarn before you start knitting. If you put your needle down before you start knitting, you're likely to lose some of your cast-on stitches, as they won't be secure until you've knitted or purled the first row. I always recommend knitting or purling a plain row before you start knitting your pattern. This row will be a wrong side row.

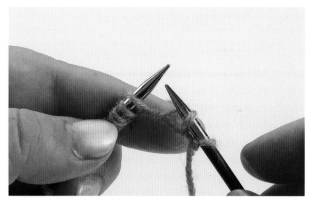

12. Two stitches have been knitted.

Working Into the Invisible Cast-On

When you are ready to undo the provisional cast-on, place the stitches back on a needle. Every other stitch will be twisted and you will have one stitch less than you cast on.

10. Carefully transfer the knitting needle to your left hand, holding onto the first stitch carefully to make sure the stitches don't start unraveling.

1. Insert the needle into the stitches and remove the waste yarn.

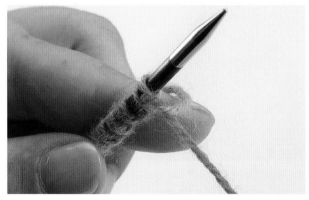

11. Holding the needle in your left hand ready to start knitting.

2. The waste yarn has been removed and the stitches are on a needle ready to knit.

Long-Tail Cast-On

This can be worked over one needle but I recommend using two needles held together. This means that you can pull each stitch tighter but every stitch will still be the same size and perfectly even. This in turn means you can cast on much more quickly. When you've finished casting on, remove one needle and the stitches will be perfectly even and loose enough to slide easily along your needle. Your cast-on edge will also be stretchier. If you are using a needle size larger than US 7 (4.5 mm), hold together one needle of the size used in the pattern and one needle in a smaller size to prevent the stitches on the first row from being too large.

Measure out a tail long enough for the number of stitches you need. There are several ways of doing this but here is how I estimate it: Wind the yarn once around your hand. This length of yarn will equal approximately 15 to 20 stitches in lace weight yarn, 10 to 15 stitches in fingering weight yarn, 10 stitches in worsted yarn, and 5 stitches in chunky. However, I do recommend allowing a bit of extra yarn, just in case. So if I need to cast on 50 stitches in worsted yarn, I wind the yarn 5 times around my hand plus a little bit extra.

Hold two needles together in your right hand. Make a slip knot and put it on the two needles.

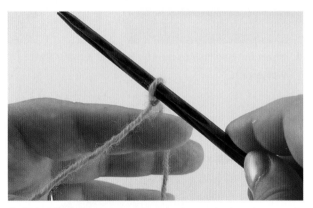

1. Take the tail over your thumb as seen in the photo and the working yarn over your index finger on your left hand.

2. Grab both the tail and the working yarn with your ring finger and little finger of your left hand and hold them tight. Turn your left hand so the palm faces you.

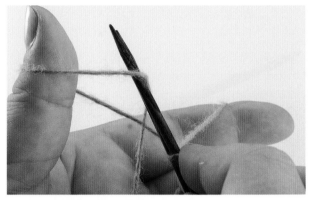

3. Move the needle toward you and under the strand that loops around your thumb.

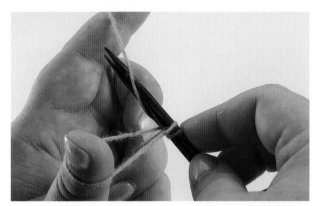

4. Take the needle outside and under the strand that goes around your index finger.

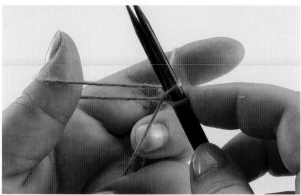

5. Take the needle through the loop that goes around your thumb, toward you.

6. Drop the loop that goes around your thumb and tighten the stitch.

You are now ready to cast on the next stitch.

7. The cast-on is complete. Pull one needle out and you're ready to knit.

Circular Cast-Ons

When starting to work a piece from the center out in the round, such as a circular or square shawl, you can use a regular cast-on but a circular cast-on looks much nicer. Below I will give you instructions for two methods that give a similar result; neither is better than the other. Try both and use the one you find easiest. Emily Ocker's Circular Cast-On requires a crochet hook, and if you are new to crochet you may find the Disappearing Loop Cast-On easier. There are also a number of YouTube videos and other online tutorials for both techniques.

Emily Ocker's Circular Cast-On

I'm not sure who Emily Ocker is or why this cast-on is named after her but from what I've read, Elizabeth Zimmerman, who was a well-known and popular hand-knit designer in the 20th century, learned this cast-on from a lady named Emily Ocker.

You will need a crochet hook in a similar size as the needles used in your pattern or a size smaller.

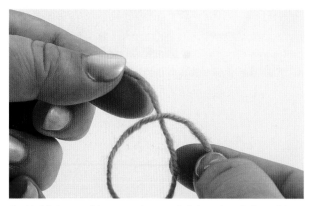

1. Hold the working yarn in your left hand and the tail in your right hand. Cross the tail in front of the working yarn to make a loop.

(continued)

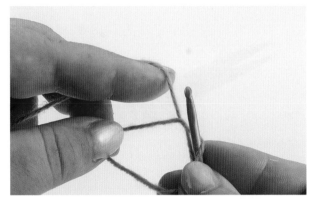

2. Tension the working yarn over your left index finger, take the crochet hook through the circle, and pull up a loop.

3. Yarn over the hook and pull it through the stitch on the hook.

4. *Take the hook through the circle and pull up a loop.

5. Yarn over the hook and pull it through the stitch on the hook.

6. Repeat from * until you have the number of stitches the pattern states. In this example, we'll use 8 stitches.

9. Rep from * until you have the stitches divided between 4 double-pointed needles and you have worked one round.

7. Slip 4 stitches onto one double-pointed needle and slip the other 4 stitches onto a second double-pointed needle.

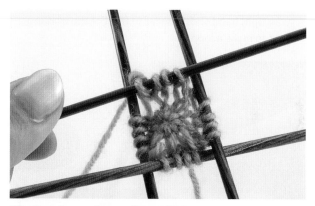

10. Start increasing as directed in your pattern.

8. *Using a new double-pointed needle, knit 2 stitches.

Emily Ocker's Circular Cast-On used in a square.

Disappearing Loop Cast-On

You will need a set of 5 double-pointed needles for this.

1. Hold the working yarn in your left hand and the tail in your right hand. Cross the tail in front of the working yarn to make a loop.

2. Take the first double-pointed needle and take the working yarn over the needle.

3. Take the needle inside the circle.

4. Take the yarn over the needle and pull it back through the circle.

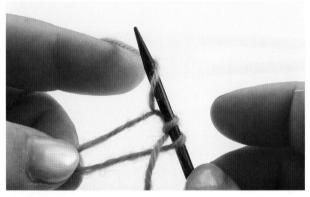

5. *Take the yarn over the needle.

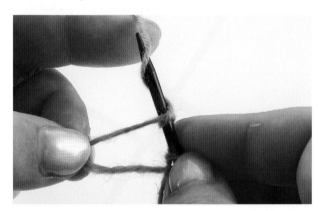

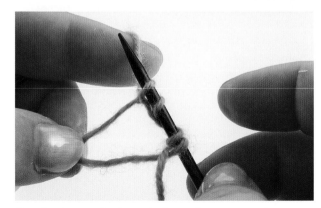

6. Take the needle through the circle, yarn over the needle, and bring it back through the circle.

7. Repeat from * until you've cast on the number of stitches the pattern directs. In this example, I am using 8 stitches.

8. Divide the stitches onto 2 double-pointed needles.

A swatch using Disappearing Loop Cast-On.

Binding off

Russian Bind-Off

This gives a stretchy bind-off, which is essential for lace knitting to allow the edge to be stretched during blocking.

1. Knit 2 stitches.

2. *Insert the left needle into the front loops of those 2 stitches and knit them together (or you can slip both stitches back to the left needle and knit them together through the back loops).

(continued)

9. Using another double-pointed needle, knit 2 stitches. Repeat until you've worked one round and the stitches are divided onto 4 double-pointed needles. Pull on the tail to tighten the circle.

Continue increasing as directed in the pattern.

3. This leaves 1 stitch on the right needle.

4. Knit 1.

Repeat from * until the correct number of stitches has been bound off. Once you've bound off the required stitches, you will be left with 1 stitch on the right needle. Break the yarn and pull it through this stitch as you would a normal bind-off.

Three-Needle Bind-Off

This is a good way of joining two pieces of knitting. You won't get a completely seamless join (as with the Kitchener stitch) but the seam will be smoother and less bulky than a regular seam.

The two pieces of knitting to be joined should each be on a separate needle. Break the yarn, leaving a long tail on the piece held at the back. You will need a third needle in the pattern size. If you don't have a spare needle in the right size, put one of the pieces to be joined on a smaller size needle so the correct size needle can be used for binding off.

The photos shown right show the three-needle bind-off being performed by a continental knitter working a Norwegian purl (with the yarn at the back in the left hand).

1. Hold the two pieces to be joined in your left hand with right sides together.

2. Insert the right needle into the first stitch on the back needle and the first stitch on the front needle purlwise and purl these 2 stitches together.

The wrong side of a piece bound off using Three-Needle Bind-Off.

3. *Insert the right needle into the next stitch on the back needle and the next stitch on the front needle purlwise and purl these 2 stitches together.

The right side of the same piece.

4. You now have 2 stitches on the right needle.

5. Lift the first stitch over the second stitch just as in a regular bind-off. You have now bound off one stitch and one stitch remains on the right needle.
Repeat from * until all the stitches have been bound off.

Sewn Bind-Off

This bind-off results in an edge that is stretchier than that of a regular bind-off but not as stretchy as the Russian Bind-Off. I like to use this bind-off for necklines, the tops of fingerless gloves/mittens/hand warmers, and socks.

Break the yarn, leaving a tail long enough to bind off all the stitches (approximately three times the length to be bound off).

Hold the knitting needle in your left hand. Thread the yarn on a blunt tapestry needle and hold it in your right hand. Every time you insert the tapestry needle into a stitch, pull the yarn all the way through.

(continued)

1. *Insert the tapestry needle into the first 2 stitches purlwise and leave both stitches on the knitting needle.

2. Insert the tapestry needle into the first stitch only knitwise and take this stitch off the knitting needle. You've now bound off one stitch.

3. Repeat from * until all the stitches have been bound off. When you come to the last 2 stitches, perform steps 1 and 2, then slip both stitches off the needle and fasten the yarn.

Several stitches bound off using a Sewn Bind-Off.

Grafting with the Kitchener Stitch

Although sometimes the instructions for Kitchener stitch include two set-up steps, I never do them. I've tested the graft with and without these steps, and I can't tell the difference, so I jump right in at step 1, as follows.

1. Hold the two pieces to be grafted, with the wrong sides together, in your left hand. Break the yarn, leaving a long tail (in the photos, I'm using a pink yarn to graft with). Thread the yarn on a blunt tapestry needle and hold in your right hand.

2. *Insert the tapestry needle into the first stitch on the front needle knitwise and take the stitch off the knitting needle.

3. Insert the tapestry needle into the next stitch on the front needle purlwise and leave this stitch on the knitting needle.

4. Insert the tapestry needle into the first stitch on the back needle purlwise and take the stitch off the knitting needle.

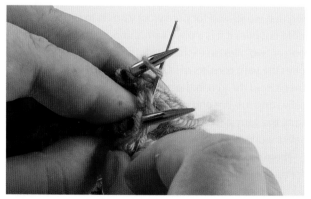

5. Insert the tapestry needle into the next stitch on the back needle knitwise and leave this stitch on the knitting needle.

6. Repeat from * until all the stitches have been grafted. For the last 2 stitches, insert the needle knitwise into the stitch on the front needle then purlwise into the stitch on the back needle and slip both stitches off the needle.

Adding Beads to Your Knitting

There are several ways to add beads to your knitting but I prefer adding them using a crochet hook, which is what I will show you here.

You need a crochet hook small enough for the bead to fit on it. I usually use a US 13 (0.75 mm) or US 15 (0.50 mm) steel crochet hook, depending on the size of the beads I'm using.

1. Place a bead on the crochet hook.

(continued)

2. Lift the stitch off the left needle using the crochet hook.

3. The stitch should sit in the hook of the crochet hook.
4. Push the bead onto the stitch.

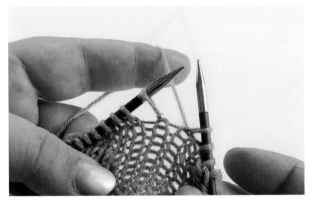

5. Place the stitch back on the left needle.

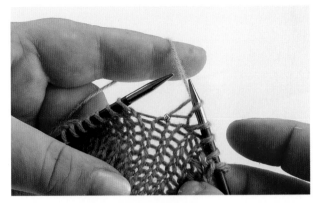

6. Knit the beaded stitch as normal.

Joining in a New Yarn

It usually looks neatest to join a new yarn at the edge. In garments that are to be seamed, this means the ends can be woven into the seams and hidden better. In shawls, scarves, and other accessories where there are no seams, I still prefer to join a new yarn at the edge. I prefer to leave the old end with enough yarn to weave it in (about 4 in. /10 cm), pull out a similar amount of the new yarn, and start knitting. Leave the two ends until you've finished knitting, then carefully weave them in. They can be woven into the edge of the fabric of shawls and other accessories quite succesfully. In items that aren't too open, it may be okay to weave in ends in a solid area of the fabric.

Alternatively, you may choose to splice the new yarn. Personally, I'm not that keen on doing it as it often makes the yarn a bit thicker for a short section. One way of splicing that works well for pure wool yarns is to separate the different plies if it is a plied yarn. Cut out a short section of one or two plies on each end (depending on how many plies the yarn consists of). Overlap the yarn so the cut ends meet. Hold the join in the palm of your hand. Add some saliva and rub the ends vigorously together in your hands until the yarn starts to felt. Continue knitting. Apparently saliva works better than water for this method.

There are other ways of splicing yarn, too. Search online for tutorials and instructions.

Short-Row Shaping

Short rows can be inserted into your knitting to create extra fabric and curves. You can use them to add bust shaping and to shape shoulders, shawls, and more. In this book, short rows are mainly used to shape the shoulders in garments and to shape crescent shawls.

In the shawls Love Hearts (page 72) and Josephine (page 133), very simple short rows are used to create their crescent shapes.

To work short rows in these two patterns, simply turn as instructed in the pattern. Turning in the middle of a row creates a gap. On the next row, work until you get to one stitch before the gap, then work a decrease into the next two stitches (the ones before and after the gap) to close it. Knit a few more stitches as instructed in the pattern and turn again.

Short rows are also used to shape the shoulders in garments, creating a smoother curve than the traditional "stair step" shoulder bind-off. Start working the short rows from the neck end of the shoulder. There are several different short-row methods and there are lots of video and written tutorials available online. Check out a few and find your favorite.

I prefer to use Wrap and Turn short rows.

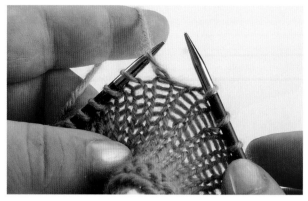

3. Slip the stitch back to the left needle.

4. Turn your knitting and work the next wrong side row.

Wrap and Turn Short Rows on a Purl Row

1. Purl to where you want to turn. Take the working yarn to the back. (If you use Norwegian purl, leave the yarn at the back.)

Wrap and Turn Short Rows on a Knit Row

1. Knit to where you want to turn. Take the working yarn to the front and slip the next stitch purlwise to the right needle.

2. Take the working yarn to the back.

2. Slip the next stitch purlwise to the right needle.

(continued)

3. Take the working yarn to the front and slip the stitch back to the left needle.

4. Turn your knitting and work the next right side row.

After you have finished working your short rows, you will work one row where you knit or purl across all the stitches and knit or purl the wrap together with the stitch it was wrapped around. This will hide the wrap from the right side of the fabric. These instructions assume that the knit row is the right side row of a stockinette fabric.

3. Knit the 2 loops together.

Pick Up and Work Wrap on a Knit Row

A wrap after it's been knitted together with the stitch it was wrapped around from the right side.

1. Knit to the first wrap. Insert the needle tip up through the wrap.

Pick Up and Work a Wrap on a Purl Row

2. Insert the needle tip into the stitch knitwise.

1. Purl to the first wrap. Tilt your knitting so you can see the knit side of the fabric. Insert the right needle tip up through the wrap.

2. Lift the wrap up and put it on the left needle in front of the stitch it was wrapped around.

3. Purl the 2 loops together.

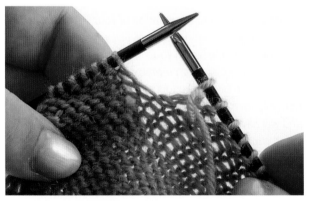

A wrap after it's been purled together with the stitch it was wrapped around from the wrong side.

Using My Patterns

The information that follows will aid in your success.

Skill Level

The patterns that follow are organized by their level of complexity, starting with what I'm calling Level 1 lace. These pieces are the easiest, employing basic lace, with repetitive lace patterning, simple shaping, and a selective use of beads. If you're new to lace or knitting with beads, you will want to pick from these patterns to develop the experience and comfort with beading and knitting lace that you'll need to move on to the patterns on the next two levels.

Level 2 pieces have slightly more complex shaping, all-over lace patterns, and a greater use of beads. The patterns Edie, Adelaide, and Christine involve quite a number of beads (a thousand or more), but the knitting and lace techniques they employ are less demanding than for the other Level 2 pieces, so if you're feeling comfortable with your beading skills but wanting a less involved lace pattern, take a look at these. When you have honed your lace *and* beading skills, you will be ready for the Level 3 pieces, which have complex shaping and lace patterning.

Substituting Yarn

Many knitters worry about substituting yarn, but it's easier than you think. Just follow a few simple rules.

First, look at the fiber content of the yarn used in the original pattern. There may be a reason why the designer has chosen a specific fiber or combination of fibers, so for a successful yarn substitution it is important to take yarn content into account. You may wish to use an alternative fiber, but before you decide take into account how that fiber behaves and how it will look in the chosen stitch pattern. For example, a lace pattern knitted in smooth silk will look very different from the same pattern knitted in brushed mohair; as the mohair is fluffy, it will fill in some of the holes in the lace.

Also, look at the yards per skein size. If the yarn has 400 yards in a 100-gram skein, choose a yarn that has the same number of yards in the same size skein.

Always knit a swatch in your new yarn to make sure it works well with the needle size and stitch pattern. And don't forget to check your gauge. Your new yarn may knit up to a different gauge than the pattern's original yarn.

In accessories such as shawls and scarves that don't have to have an exact fit, substituting yarn is relatively simple. Simply choose an alternative yarn. I recommend knitting a swatch to make sure you are happy with the new yarn and needle size combination. Always block a lace swatch before making a decision on whether or not you like the resulting fabric.

If exact size is not important, then you can choose a yarn in a different weight. For example, the two circular shawls in this book are knitted in lace weight yarn; if you choose to work them in a worsted yarn, they will become warm afghans instead of delicate shawls, which is fine, so long as you know that's what the outcome will be. Also take into account if you choose to knit the item in a different yarn weight, you may need more yardage than the pattern states.

Swatching—It's About More Than Gauge

Many knitters skip swatching, thinking it's a waste of time. Actually, it's a very important part of knitting up a pattern. Swatching will tell you many things about your chosen project and the yarn you are using.

First, it's important to knit a swatch to check your gauge. Before you start your swatch, check which stitch pattern the swatch is knitted in. Always wash and block a swatch before measuring gauge.

For garments, gauge is important for good fit. If your gauge is off, the garment won't fit. I like to double-check gauge on my garments. After a few inches of knitting, I will measure the width and double-check against the measurements in the pattern to make sure I'm still on track.

Swatching will also tell you if you like the yarn you've chosen and if it works with the stitch pattern used in the pattern. If you're unsure of a specific yarn, get a small amount (like one ball) and knit a swatch before you go ahead and buy the full amount needed for the project (of course, making sure the balance of the yarn is from the same dye lot).

If the project includes techniques that are new to you, it's a good idea to practice them on a swatch first. This will help you iron out any problems before you start on the actual project.

Many knitters think that gauge doesn't matter when it comes to accessories like shawls and scarves, and they're partly right. The main problem with not getting gauge is that you may use more yarn than the pattern states. So if you decide to throw caution to the wind and not swatch, then do make sure you have more yarn available. Not knitting to the correct gauge will also affect the final size of the item.

Shawl Construction

There are many different ways to knit a shawl. For example, triangles can be worked sideways, from the top down with decreases along the sides, from the top down with central spine increases, from the bottom up, and in other ways.

Some of the shaping used for shawls can take a bit of getting used to. Sometimes, reading through the pattern you can't immediately see how the shape will emerge. Trust the pattern, follow the instructions, and look at the shape emerging from your needles. This will help you understand various types of shawl construction.

The Beads

In each pattern I specify the number, size, and color of bead for the project. In parentheses I include the source for the beads used in the project and its color and number where appropriate. Living in the U.K. as I do, all of my online sources are located here as well. For readers in the U.S., Canada, and elsewhere, you may want to find your own source, matching the color as best you can.

Reading Charts

Charts are a visual representation of your knitting and show what your knitting will look like when you look at it with the right side facing you.

Each square on a chart represents one stitch, and charts are read from bottom to top. Right-side rows, which are normally rows 1, 3, 5, 7, 9, etc., are read from right to left and will have the row number on the right side of the chart. Wrong-side rows, normally rows 2, 4, 6, 8, etc., are read from left to right and will have the row number on the left side of the chart. When working in the round, all round numbers are on the right side of the chart.

On many lace patterns, every other row is a "rest" row, which means it's a plain knit or a plain purl row. Plain rows are quite often taken out of the chart. This means that only right side rows are charted. This will be noted and the pattern will tell you how to work the wrong side rows.

Pattern repeats are shown inside red borders on the chart and in [ ] in the written instructions. In this book, I've included both the chart and written directions for the chart so that you can use what you're most comfortable with. I do encourage you to use the charts, though. With experience, reading them will become second nature and you'll prefer them to written instructions.

All charts have a key, or legend, that will tell you what the different symbols mean. Unfortunately, there is no international standard system for knitting chart symbols, so each designer/publisher has their own standard symbols. Always check the key before starting.

Blocking

Blocking is essential for your lace project to look its best. Before you start blocking, make sure you have at hand:

- An area large enough for your finished item to be laid out flat.
- A towel to squeeze water out of the garment.
- A towel, blanket, blocking mat, or something similar to keep the surface underneath dry.
- Lots of pins.
- Optional: Blocking wires. They make the job easier but are not essential.

To block the piece:
1. Soak the piece of knitting in lukewarm water with some wool wash (or fabric conditioner) until wet (about 10 minutes is long enough). Lift the knitting carefully out of the water and gently squeeze out excess liquid. Put the knitting in a towel, roll the towel up and press to remove as much water as possible.
2. Lay the piece out flat, stretching it to the shape and size you want (measure if necessary). Don't be afraid to stretch the piece, especially if it's an accessory. With garments, check the measurements in the pattern.
3. Insert blocking wires if using and pin in place. If not using blocking wires, pin in place. Start pinning in the corners first, then add pins along the straight edges. Stretch and smooth out the lace while pinning it. If you want scalloped edges or points, use one pin for each point.
4. Leave to dry completely.
5. Unpin the piece when dry. Once it is dry and unpinned, your knitting will relax a little bit and your item is unlikely to stay the size it was blocked to. Therefore I recommend stretching it as much as possible during blocking (but if it's a garment, then do check final measurements as per pattern).

Abbreviations

B	add bead and knit
CCO	cable cast-on
CO	cast on
dpn(s)	double-pointed needle(s)
est	established
foll	following
k	knit
kfb	knit in front and back of st
kwise	knitwise
LH	left hand
m	marker
m1	make a st by lifting strand between 2 sts and k tbl
p	purl
patt	pattern
pm	place marker
psso	pass slipped st over
pwise	purlwise
RBO	Russian Bind-Off
rep	repeat
RH	right hand
RS	right side

sl1, k2tog, psso	slip 1 st knitwise, knit the next 2 sts tog, pass slipped st over—2 sts dec'd
sl, k2, psso	slip 1 stitch, k2, pass slipped st over 2 knitted stitches—1 st dec'd
SJ	single join
sl	slip
sm	slip marker
ssk	slip 1 st knitwise, slip another st knitwise, insert left needle into front of both sts and knit together—1 st dec'd
sssk	one at a time, slip 3 sts knitwise, insert left needle into front of 3 sts, knit together—2 sts dec'd
ssp	slip 1 st knitwise , slip another st knitwise, slip both sts back to left needle, purl together tbl—1 st dec'd
st(s)	stitch(es)
st st	stockinette stitch
tbl	through back loop
tog	together
w&t	wrap and turn
WS	wrong side
wyif	with yarn in front
2x2 rib	k2, p2

Gillian

This delicate poncho is perfect for when you want to wear beautiful lace, but don't want it slipping off your shoulders or blowing around in the breeze. Beads are added to a medallion lace pattern for a bit of extra shimmer.

Level 1

FINISHED MEASUREMENTS

Width: 14 (17^1/$_2$, 21) in./35.5 (44.5, 53) cm
Length: 65 (65, 71) in./165 (165, 180) cm

YARN

Sweet Georgia Merino Silk Lace, lace weight #0 yarn, 50% fine merino wool/50% silk, 765 yd./700 m, 3.5 oz./100 g
• 2 (2, 2) skeins Riptide

NEEDLES AND OTHER MATERIALS

• US 4 (3.5 mm) knitting needles
• 508 (676, 904) coppery charcoal size 8 seed beads (debbieabrahamsbeads.co.uk, #605 Slick)
• US 15 (0.50 mm) steel crochet hook (for adding beads)
• Stitch markers
• Tapestry needle

GAUGE

18.5 sts x 28 rows in Chart B patt after blocking = 4 in./10 cm square
Be sure to check your gauge!

Notes

• Poncho is worked flat as a rectangle, then folded in half and seamed together partially along one edge after blocking to create the opening for the head. It can be made longer or shorter by working more or fewer repeats of the lace pattern in Chart B.
• See page 17 for a photo tutorial on Russian Bind-Off.

Poncho Edging

CO 67, (83, 99) sts.
Row 1 (RS): K to end.
Row 2 (WS): Sl wyif, k to end.
Rep Row 2 four more times (6 rows worked in garter stitch).

Work Chart A

Row 1 (RS): Work Row 1 of Chart A, working patt rep 3 (4, 5) times.
Row 2 (WS): Work Row 2 of Chart A.
Continue to work in patt through all 10 rows of Chart A once.

Work Chart B

Row 1 (RS): Work Row 1 of Chart B, working patt rep 3 (4, 5) times.
Row 2 (WS): Work Row 2 of Chart B.
Continue to work in patt through all 32 rows of Chart B a total of 14 (14, 15) times.

Work Chart C

Row 1 (RS): Work Row 1 of Chart C, working patt rep 3 (4, 5) times.
Row 2 (WS): Work Row 2 of Chart C.
Continue to work in patt through all 12 rows of Chart C once.
Next row: Sl wyif, k to end.
Rep last row 5 more times.
BO using Russian Bind-Off.

Finishing

Weave in all loose ends. Block poncho. When dry, fold rectangle in half with RS facing. Starting where the corners come together, with the tapestry needle and a length of yarn, stitch along the edge, allowing enough room to pull the poncho over your head. Break off and weave in the ends.

Chart A

Pattern repeat is in [ ].
Row 1 (RS): Sl wyif, k8, [k6, k2tog, yo, k1, yo, ssk, k5], k10.
Row 2 and WS rows: Sl wyif, k3, p to last 4 sts, k4.
Row 3: Sl wyif, k8, [k5, k2tog, yo, k3, yo, ssk, k4], k10.

Key

☐	RS: knit / WS: purl
○	RS: yo
╱	RS: k2tog
╲	RS: ssk
∧	RS: sl1, k2tog, psso
B	add bead and knit
V̇	RS/WS: slip purlwise with yarn in front
●	WS: knit
☐	pattern repeat

Chart A

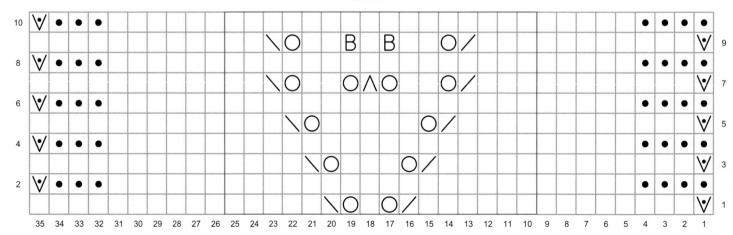

Row 5: Sl wyif, k8, [k4, k2tog, yo, k5, yo, ssk, k3], k10.

Row 7: Sl wyif, k8, [k3, k2tog, yo, k2, yo, sl1, k2tog, psso, yo, k2, yo, ssk, k2], k10.

Row 9: Sl wyif, k8, [k3, k2tog, yo, k2, B, k1, B, k2, yo, ssk, k2], k10.

Row 10: Sl wyif, k3, p to last 4 sts, k4.

Chart B

Pattern repeat is in [ ].

Row 1 (RS): Sl wyif, k8, [k3, k2tog, yo, k2, yo, sl1, k2tog, psso, yo, k2, yo, ssk, k2], k10.

Row 2 and all WS rows: Sl wyif, k3, p to last 4 sts, k4.

Row 3: Sl wyif, k8, [k3, k2tog, yo, k2, B, k1, B, k2, yo, ssk, k2], k10.

Row 5: Sl wyif, k8, [k3, k2tog, yo, k2, yo, sl1, k2tog, psso, yo, k2, yo, ssk, k2], k10.

Row 7: Sl wyif, k6, k2tog, yo, [k1, yo, ssk, k2, yo, ssk, k3, k2tog, yo, k2, k2tog, yo], k1, yo, ssk, k7.

Row 9: Sl wyif, k5, k2tog, yo, k1, [(k2, yo, ssk) 2 times, k1, k2tog, yo, k2, k2tog, yo, k1], k2, yo, ssk, k6.

Row 11: Sl wyif, k4, k2tog, yo, k2, [k3, yo, ssk, k2, yo, sl1, k2tog, psso, yo, k2, k2tog, yo, k2], k3, yo, ssk, k5.

Row 13: Sl wyif, k3, k2tog, yo, k2, yo, [sl1, k2tog, psso, yo, k2, yo, ssk, k5, k2tog, yo, k2, yo], sl1, k2tog, psso, yo, k2, yo, ssk, k4.

(continued)

Chart B

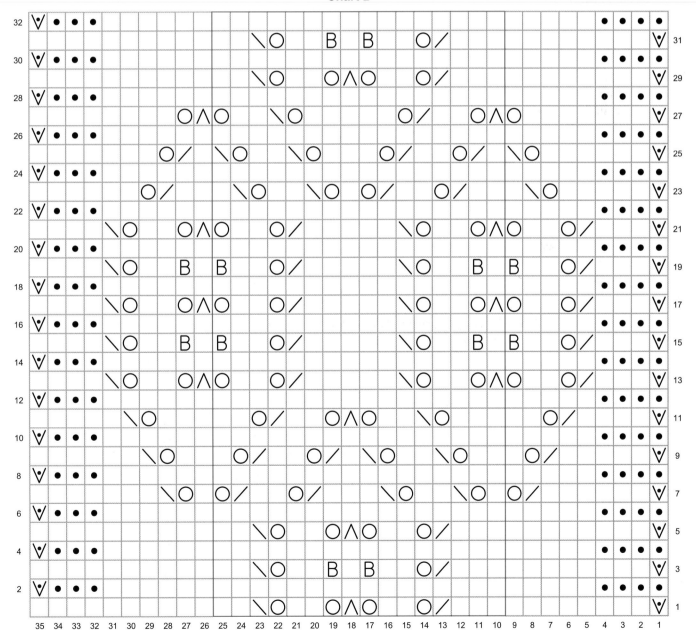

Row 15: Sl wyif, k3, k2tog, yo, k2, B, (k1, B, k2, yo, ssk, k5, k2tog, yo, k2, B), k1, B, k2, yo, ssk, k4.

Row 17: Sl wyif, k3, k2tog, yo, k2, yo, [sl1, k2tog, psso, yo, k2, yo, ssk, k5, k2tog, yo, k2, yo], sl1, k2tog, psso, yo, k2, yo, ssk, k4.

Row 19: Sl wyif, k3, k2tog, yo, k2, B, [k1, B, k2, yo, ssk, k5, k2tog, yo, k2, B], k1, B, k2, yo, ssk, k4.

Row 21: Sl wyif, k3, k2tog, yo, k2, yo, [sl1, k2tog, psso, yo, k2, yo, ssk, k5, k2tog, yo, k2, yo], sl1, k2tog, psso, yo, k2, yo, ssk, k4.

Row 23: Sl wyif, k5, yo, ssk, k1, [(k2, k2tog, yo) 2 times, k1, yo, ssk, k2, yo, ssk, k1], k2, k2tog, yo, k6.

Row 25: Sl wyif, k6, yo, ssk, [k1, k2tog, yo, k2, k2tog, yo, k3, yo, ssk, k2, yo, ssk], k1, k2tog, yo, k7.

Row 27: Sl wyif, k7, yo, [sl1, k2tog, psso, yo, k2, k2tog, yo, k5, yo, ssk, k2, yo], sl1, k2tog, psso, yo, k8.

Row 29: Sl wyif, k8, [k3, k2tog, yo, k2, yo, sl1, k2tog, psso, yo, k2, yo, ssk, k2], k10.

Row 31: Sl wyif, k8, [k3, k2tog, yo, k2, B, k1, B, k2, yo, ssk, k2], k10.

Row 32: Sl wyif, k3, p to last 4 sts, k4.

Chart C

Pattern repeat is in [ ].

Row 1 (RS): Sl wyif, k8, [k3, k2tog, yo, k2, yo, sl1, k2tog, psso, yo, k2, yo, ssk, k2], k10.

Row 2 and all WS rows: Sl wyif, k3, p to last 4 sts, k4.

Row 3: Sl wyif, k8, [k3, k2tog, yo, k2, B, k1, B, k2, yo, ssk, k2], k10.

Row 5: Sl wyif, k8, [k3, k2tog, yo, k2, yo, sl1, k2tog, psso, yo, k2, yo, ssk, k2], k10.

Row 7: Sl wyif, k8, [k5, yo, ssk, k3, k2tog, yo, k4], k10.

Row 9: Sl wyif, k8, [k6, yo, ssk, k1, k2tog, yo, k5], k10.

Row 11: Sl wyif, k8, [k7, yo, sl1, k2tog, psso, yo, k6], k10.

Row 12: Sl wyif, k3, p to last 4 sts, k4.

Chart C

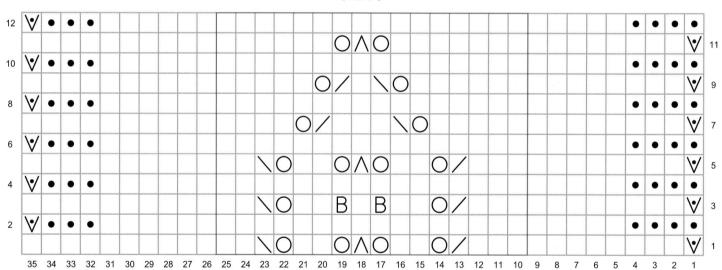

Key

☐	RS: knit / WS: purl
○	RS: yo
╱	RS: k2tog
╲	RS: ssk
⋀	RS: sl1, k2tog, psso
B	add bead and knit
V̇	RS/WS: slip purlwise with yarn in front
●	WS: knit
☐	pattern repeat

Eden

Eden uses a luxurious, hand-dyed merino blend yarn, which is soft and warm around your neck. Beads at the bottom of the cowl add weight to a drapey fabric. It's the perfect accessory to wear under your winter coat as it will keep your neck warm without adding bulk.

Skill Level

Level 1

Notes

- Row 1 of Chart B reduces the stitch count from 20 sts per patt repeat to 18 sts per patt repeat (126 sts). Row 3 further reduces the stitch count from 18 sts per patt repeat to 16 sts per patt repeat (112 sts).
- See page 17 for a photo tutorial on Russian Bind-Off.

FINISHED MEASUREMENTS
Circumference at top: 27 in./68.5 cm
Length, top to bottom: 17 in./43 cm

YARN
Lorna's Laces Solemate, fingering weight #1 yarn, 55% superwash merino wool/30% Outlast viscose/15% nylon, 425 yd./388 m, 3.5 oz./100 g
- 1 skein #1112 Ascot

NEEDLES AND OTHER MATERIALS
- US 6 (4 mm) circular needle, 24 in./60 cm long
- 112 light green 4 mm miracle beads
- US 13 (0.75 mm) steel crochet hook (for adding beads)
- Tapestry needle

GAUGE
21 sts x 30 rows in Chart B patt after blocking = 4 in./10 cm square
Be sure to check your gauge!

Cowl

CO 140 sts. Join to work in the rnd, being careful not to twist sts. Place a stitch marker to indicate beg of rnd.

Rnd 1: K to end.

Rnd 2: P to end.

Rep Rnds 1–2 once more.

Next rnd: Work Row 1 of Chart A, working patt repeat 7 times.

Continue to work in patt through all 12 rows of Chart A once.

Next rnd: Work Row 1 of Chart B, working patt repeat 7 times—126 sts.

Continue to work in patt through all 4 rows of Chart B once—112 sts.

Next rnd: Work Row 1 of Chart C, working patt repeat 7 times.

Continue to work in patt through all 4 rows of Lace patt C 25 times.

Next rnd: P to end.

Next rnd: K to end.

Rep last 2 rnds once more.

BO using the Russian Bind-Off.

Finishing

Weave in all loose ends. Block scarf.

Chart A

Row 1: B, yo, ssk, k3, k2tog, yo, B, k4, yo, sl1, k2tog, psso, yo, k4.

Row 2 and all even-numbered rnds: K to end.

Row 3: K1, B, yo, ssk, k1, k2tog, yo, B, k5, yo, sl1, k2tog, psso, yo, k4.

(continued)

Key

☐ knit		⋀ sl1, k2tog, psso
◯ yo		B add bead and knit
╱ k2tog		
╲ ssk		

Chart A

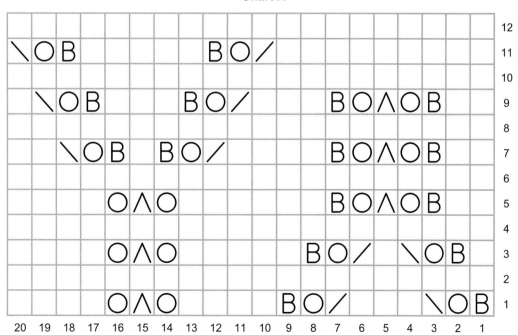

Row 5: K2, B, yo, sl1, k2tog, psso, yo, B, k6, yo, sl1, k2tog, psso, yo, k4.

Row 7: K2, B, yo, sl1, k2tog, psso, yo, B, k4, k2tog, yo, B, k1, B, yo, ssk, k2.

Row 9: K2, B, yo, sl1, k2tog, psso, yo, B, k3, k2tog, yo, B, k3, B, yo, ssk, k1.

Row 11: K9, k2tog, yo, B, k5, B, yo, ssk.

Row 12: K to end.

Chart B

Row 1: K1, ssk, yo, sl1, k2tog, psso, yo, k2tog, (k1, yo, ssk) 2 times, k1, k2tog, yo, k1, yo, ssk.

Rows 2 and 4: K to end.

Row 3: K1, ssk, (k1, k2tog) 2 times, yo, k2, yo, sl1, k2tog, psso, yo, k2, k2tog, yo.

Chart C

Row 1: K1, yo, sl1, k2tog, psso, yo, (k1, yo, ssk) 2 times, k1, k2tog, yo, k1, yo, ssk.

Rows 2 and 4: K to end.

Row 3: K5, k2tog, yo, k2, yo, sl1, k2tog, psso, yo, k2, k2tog, yo.

Chart B

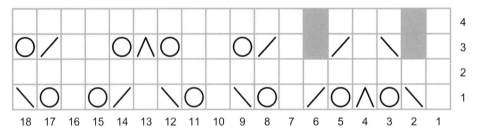

Chart C

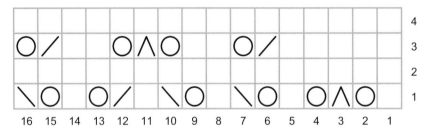

Key

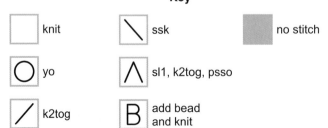

	knit		ssk		no stitch
◯	yo	⋀	sl1, k2tog, psso		
╱	k2tog	B	add bead and knit		

Alexia

Alexia is worked sideways to create a shallow triangular shawl, and can easily be adjusted to work with different yarn amounts. Work the first half until you've used half your available yarn, then start the second half. The all-over beaded lace pattern adds elegance to a piece that can be worn as a shawl or as a scarf.

Skill Level

Level 1

Notes

- For the first stitch of every RS row, attach the bead, then slip the stitch purlwise with the yarn in front.
- See page 17 for a photo tutorial on Russian Bind-Off.

FINISHED MEASUREMENTS
Length: 74^1/$_2$ in./189 cm
Depth (center back): 32 in./81 cm

YARN
Cascade Yarns Forest Hills, super fine #1 yarn, 51% silk/49% merino wool, 785 yd./717.5 m, 3.5 oz./100 g
- 1 skein #09 Nugget Gold

NEEDLES AND OTHER MATERIALS
- US 4 (3.5 mm) straight or circular needles
- 274 gold-brown rainbow size 8 seed beads (thebeadroom.co.uk, #648)
- US 15 (0.50 mm) steel crochet hook (for adding beads)
- Tapestry needle

GAUGE
18 sts x 28 rows in Chart A patt after blocking = 4 in./10 cm square
Be sure to check your gauge!

SPECIAL STITCHES
Sssk: One at a time, slip 3 sts knitwise, insert left needle into front of sts, ktog—2 sts dec'd.

Cast On

CO 13 sts.
Knit one row.

First Half

Row 1 (RS): Work Row 1 of Chart A, working patt rep
once—1 st inc'd.
Continue to work in patt through all 12 rows of Chart A for
a total of 22 times—145 sts.

Second Half

Row 1 (RS): Work Row 1 of Chart B, working patt rep 22
times—1 st dec'd.
Continue to work in patt through all 12 rows of Chart B for
a total of 22 times—13 sts.
BO using Russian Bind-Off.

Finishing

Weave in loose ends. Block shawl.

Chart A

Pattern repeat is in [ ].
Row 1 (RS): B then sl st wyif, k3, yo, B, [yo, k4, k2tog], k2.
Row 2 (WS): Sl wyif, k1, [p6], p2, k4.
Row 3: B then sl st wyif, k3, yo, k2, [B, yo, k3, k2tog], k2.
Row 4: Sl wyif, k1, [p6], p3, k4.
Row 5: B then sl st wyif, k3, yo, k3, [k1, B, yo, k2, k2tog], k2.
Row 6: Sl wyif, k1, [p6], p4, k2, (yo) 3 times, k2.
Row 7: B then sl st wyif, k2, k tbl, k3, yo, k4, [k2, B, yo, k1,
k2tog], k2.
Row 8: Sl wyif, k1, [p6], p5, k2, k tbl, k1, k tbl, k2.
Row 9: B then sl st wyif, k6, yo, k5, [k3, B, yo, k2tog], k2.
Row 10: Sl wyif, k1, [p6], p6, k7.
Row 11: RBO 3 times, k3, yo, k6, [k4,B, k1], k2.
Row 12: Sl wyif, k1, [p6], p7, k4.

Key

	RS: knit WS: purl		slip purlwise with yarn in front		Russian bind-off
/	k2tog	●	WS: knit	X	st left from RBO
B	add bead and knit	Ω	RS/WS: k tbl		pattern repeat
O	yo				

Chart A

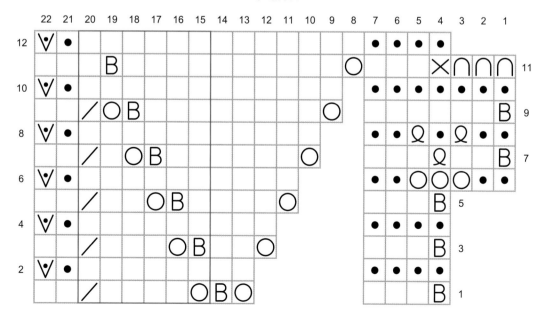

Chart B

Pattern repeat is in [ ].

Row 1 (RS): B then sl wyif, k2, yo, sssk, k4, B, [yo, k4, k2tog], k2.

Row 2 (WS): Sl wyif, k1, [p6], k3.

Row 3: B then sl wyif, k2, yo, sssk, k4, [B, yo, k3, k2tog], k2.

Row 4: Sl wyif, k1, [p6], p5, k3.

Row 5: B then sl wyif, k2, yo, sssk, k3, [k1, B, yo, k2, k2tog], k2.

Row 6: Sl wyif, k1, [p6], p4, k1, (yo) 3 times, k2.

Row 7: B then sl wyif, k2, k tbl, k2, yo, sssk, k2, [k2, B, yo, k1, k2tog], k2.

Row 8: Sl wyif, k1, [p6], p3, (k1, k tbl) 2 times, k2.

Row 9: B then sl wyif, k5, yo, sssk, k1, [k3, B, yo, k2tog], k2.

Row 10: Sl wyif, k1, [p6], p2, k6.

Row 11: RBO 3 times, k2, yo, sssk, [k4, B, k1], k2.

Row 12: Sl wyif, k1, [p6], p1, k3.

Key

RS: knit / WS: purl	Ω RS/WS: k tbl
/ k2tog	sssk
B add bead and knit	∩ Russian bind-off
O yo	X st left from RBO
V slip purlwise with yarn in front	pattern repeat
● WS: knit	

Chart B

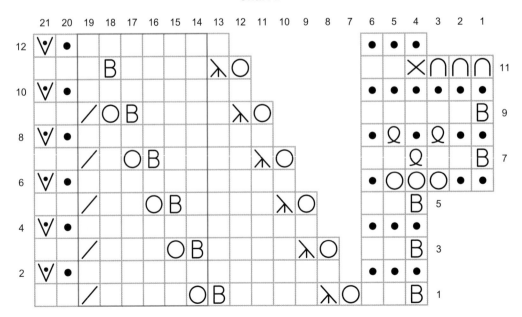

Macy

Elizabeth Zimmerman is credited with inventing the pi shawl, which has become very popular in recent years. Pi is the ratio of a circle's circumference to its diameter and in a pi shawl, the ratio of a shawl's intended circumference to its diameter dictates the spacing of the increase rounds. In Macy, I've used this formula to create a half circle, which is quicker to knit than a full circular shawl. The simple lace pattern is complemented by boldly colored miracle beads. The shawl is finished off with an edging that is knitted on at the end.

Skill Level

Level 1

Notes

- In Charts A and B, only the RS rows are charted. See pattern for WS rows.
- See page 17 for a photo tutorial on Russian Bind-Off.

FINISHED MEASUREMENTS
Width: 49 in./125.5 cm
Depth: 21 in./53.5 cm

YARN
Classic Elite Yarns Alpaca Sox, fingering weight #1 yarn, 60% alpaca/20% merino wool/20% nylon, 450 yd./411 m, 3.5 oz./100 g
- 1 skein #1832 Cereza

NEEDLES AND OTHER MATERIALS
- US 5 (3.75 mm) circular needle, 32 in./80 cm long
- 39 red 6 mm miracle beads
- US 13 (0.75 mm) steel crochet hook (for adding beads)
- Tapestry needle

GAUGE
20 sts x 24 rows in Chart B patt after blocking= 4 in./10 cm square
Be sure to check your gauge!

Cast On and Increases

CO 6 sts.

Knit one row.

Row 1 (RS): Sl wyif, k1, (yo, k1) 2 times, yo, k2—3 sts inc.

Row 2 and all WS rows: Sl wyif, k1, p to last 2 sts, k2.

Row 3: Sl wyif, k1, (yo, k1) 5 times, yo, k2—6 sts inc'd.

Rows 5 and 7: Sl wyif, k to end.

Row 9: Sl wyif, k1, (yo, k1) 11 times, yo, k2—12 sts inc'd.

Rows 11 and 13: Sl wyif, k to end.

Row 15: Sl wyif, k1, (yo, k1) 23 times, yo, k2—24 sts inc'd.

Rows 17, 19, 21, 23, and 25: Sl wyif, k to end.

Row 27: Sl wyif, k1, (yo, k1) 47 times, yo, k2—48 sts inc'd.

Row 29: Sl wyif, k to end—99 sts.

Work Chart A

Row 1 (RS): Work Row 1 of Chart A, working patt rep 10 times.

Row 2 and all WS rows: Sl wyif, k1, p to last 2 sts, k2.

Continue to work in patt through all 4 rows of Chart A a total of 7 times.

Next row (RS): Sl wyif, k to end.

Next row (WS): Sl wyif, k1, p to last 2 sts, k2.

Next row: Sl wyif, k1, (yo, k1) 95 times, yo, k2—195 sts.

Next row: Sl wyif, k1, p to last 2 sts, k2.

Next row: Sl wyif, k to end.

Next row: Sl wyif, k1, p to last 2 sts, k2.

Work Chart B

Row 1 (RS): Work Row 1 of Chart B, working patt rep 19 times.

Row 2 and all WS rows: Sl wyif, k1, p to last 2 sts, k2.

Continue to work in patt through all 8 rows of Chart B a total of 6 times.

Work Chart C

Row 1 (RS): Work Row 1 of Chart C, working patt rep 19 times.

Row 2 (WS): Sl wyif, k1, p to last 2 sts, k2.

Row 3: Work Row 3 of Chart C, working patt rep 19 times.

Row 4: Work Row 4 of Chart C, working patt rep 19 times.

Continue to work in patt through all 14 rows of Chart C once.

Leave sts on needle, do not bind off.

Edging

CO 11 sts on a separate needle.

Knit one row of edging sts. *The edging is worked in garter stitch.*

Slip these sts onto main needle so they sit in front of sts remaining from the shawl. You will knit across the edge sts, then knit the last edge st tog with 1 st from the shawl on every RS row.

Row 1 (RS): Work Row 1 of Chart D, k last st of edging tog with 1 st from shawl (single join).

Row 2 (WS): Work Row 2 of Chart D.

Row 3: Work Row 3 of Chart D, k last st of edging tog with 1 st from shawl (single join).

Row 4: Work Row 4 of Chart D.

Continue to work in patt through all 30 rows of Chart D a total of 13 times.

BO using Russian Bind-Off.

Finishing

Weave in loose ends. Block shawl.

Chart A

Pattern repeat is in [ ].

Row 1 (RS): Sl wyif, k4, [(ssk) 2 times, k2, yo, k1, yo, k2], k4.

Row 3: Sl wyif, k4, [(ssk) 2 times, yo, k3, yo, k2], k4.

Chart B

Row 1 (RS): Sl wyif, k1, [k1, yo, k3, sl1, k2tog, psso, k3, yo], k3.

Row 3: Sl wyif, k1, [k2, yo, k2, sl1, k2tog, psso, k2, yo, k1], k3.

Row 5: Sl wyif, k1, [k3, yo, k1, sl1, k2tog, psso, k1, yo, k2], k3.

Row 7: Sl wyif, k1, [k4, yo, sl1, k2tog, psso, yo, k3], k3.

Chart C

Pattern repeat is in [ ].

Row 1 (RS): Sl wyif, k to end.

Row 2 (WS): Sl wyif, k1, p to last 2 sts, k2.

Row 3: Sl wyif, k1, [(k1, k2tog, (yo) 2 times, ssk) 2 times], k3.

Row 4: Sl wyif, k1, p1, [p2, p1 tbl, p4, p1 tbl, p2], k2.

Row 5: Sl wyif, k to end.

Row 6: Sl wyif, k1, p to last 2 sts, k2.

Row 7: Sl wyif, k1, [(B, k4) 2 times], B, k2.

Row 8: Sl wyif, k1, p to last 2 sts, k2.

Row 9: Sl wyif, k to end.

Row 10: Sl wyif, k1, p to last 2 sts, k2.

Row 11: Sl wyif, k1, [(k1, k2tog, (yo) 2 times, ssk) 2 times], k3.

Row 12: Sl wyif, k1, p1, [p2, p1 tbl, p4, p1 tbl, p2], k2.

Row 13: Sl wyif, k to end.

Row 14: Sl wyif, k1, p to last 2 sts, k2.

Key

RS: knit WS: purl	m1	sl1, k2tog, psso
yo	slip purlwise with yarn in front	pattern repeat
RS/WS: k2tog	RS: purl WS: knit	add bead and knit
single join	p tbl	
ssk	k tbl	

Chart A

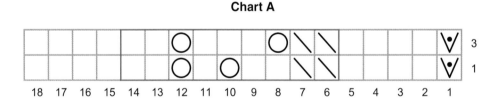

Chart B

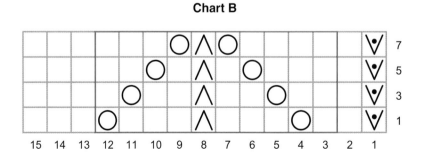

Chart D

Row 1 (RS): Sl wyif, k1, m1, k5, k2tog, yo, k1, SJ.

Row 2 (WS): Sl wyif, k2tog, yo, k9.

Row 3: Sl wyif, k1, m1, k2tog, (yo) 2 times, ssk, k2, k2tog, yo, k1, SJ.

Row 4: Sl wyif, k2tog, yo, k5, k tbl, k4.

Row 5: Sl wyif, k1, m1, k7, k2tog, yo, k1, SJ.

Row 6: Sl wyif, k2tog, yo, k11.

Row 7: Sl wyif, k1, m1, (k2tog, (yo) 2 times, ssk) 2 times, k2tog, yo, k1, SJ.

Row 8: Sl wyif, k2tog, yo, (k3, k tbl) 2 times, k4.

Row 9: Sl wyif, k1, m1, k9, k2tog, yo, k1, SJ.

Row 10: Sl wyif, k2tog, yo, k13.

Row 11: Sl wyif, k1, m1, (k2tog, (yo) 2 times, ssk) 2 times, k2, k2tog, yo, k1, SJ.

Row 12: Sl wyif, k2tog, yo, k5, k tbl, k3, k tbl, k4.

Row 13: Sl wyif, k1, m1, k11, k2tog, yo, k1, SJ.

Row 14: Sl wyif, k2tog, yo, k15.

Row 15: Sl wyif, k1, (k2tog, (yo) 2 times, ssk) 3 times, k2tog, yo, k1, SJ.

Row 16: Sl wyif, k2tog, yo, (k3, k tbl) 3 times, k3.

Row 17: Sl wyif, ssk, k11, k2tog, yo, k1, SJ.

Row 18: Sl wyif, k2tog, yo, k14.

Row 19: Sl wyif, ssk, (k2tog, (yo) 2 times, ssk) 2 times, k2, k2tog, yo, k1, SJ.

Row 20: Sl wyif, k2tog, yo, k5, k tbl, k3, k tbl, k3.

Row 21: Sl wyif, ssk, k9, k2tog, yo, k1, SJ.

Row 22: Sl wyif, k2tog, yo, k12.

Row 23: Sl wyif, ssk, (k2tog, (yo) 2 times, ssk) 2 times, k2tog, yo, k1, SJ.

Row 24: Sl wyif, k2tog, yo, (k3, k tbl) 2 times, k3.

Row 25: Sl wyif, ssk, k7, k2tog, yo, k1, SJ.

Row 26: Sl wyif, k2tog, yo, k10.

Row 27: Sl wyif, ssk, k2tog, (yo) 2 times, ssk, k2, k2tog, yo, k1, SJ.

Row 28: Sl wyif, k2tog, yo, k5, k tbl, k3.

Row 29: Sl wyif, ssk, k5, k2tog, yo, k1, SJ.

Row 30: Sl wyif, k2tog, yo, k8.

Chart D

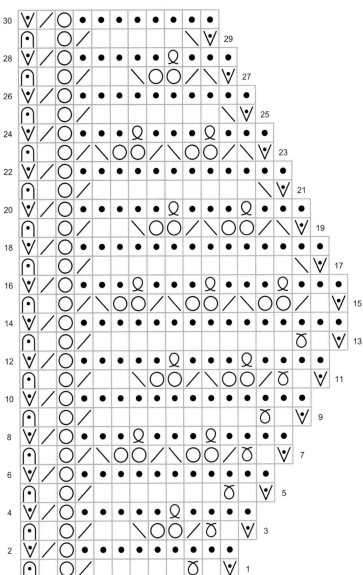

Chart C

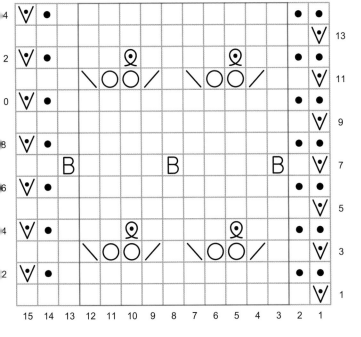

Chantelle

This beautiful waistcoat has front panels that drape like flowing water. A wavy lace pattern with beads decorates the front, with a simpler lace pattern on the back.

FINISHED MEASUREMENTS

NOTE: Use the Back Width measurement to choose a size.
Size: Small (Medium, Large)
Back length: 19 (20^1/$_2$, 22^1/$_2$) in./48 (52, 57) cm
Back width: 14 (16, 17^1/$_2$) in./35.5 (40.5, 44.5) cm
Front length: 19^1/$_2$ (20^1/$_2$, 21^1/$_4$) in./49.5 (52, 54) cm

YARN

Sublime Baby Cashmere Merino Silk, super fine weight #1 yarn, 75% extra fine merino wool/20% silk/5% cashmere, 184 yd./170 m, 1.75 oz./50 g
• 5 (6, 7) skeins #0100 Paddle

NEEDLES AND OTHER MATERIALS

• US 5 (3.75 mm) knitting needles
• 160 (184, 206) blue size 6 Japanese glass seed beads (thebeadroom.co.uk, #633 Blue Rainbow)
• US 13 (0.75 mm) steel crochet hook (for adding beads)
• Waste yarn
• Tapestry needle

GAUGE

22 sts x 41 rows in Chart A patt after blocking = 4 in./10 cm square
Be sure to check your gauge!

SPECIAL STITCHES

Cable Cast-On: Insert RH needle between first 2 sts on LH needle, wrap yarn around needle and pull through to create a new st. Place new st on LH needle.

Skill Level
Level 1

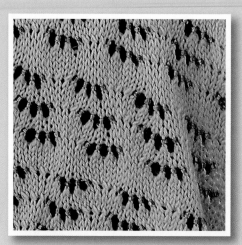

Notes

• This waistcoat is worked in one piece, starting at the center back with a provisional cast-on. Any provisional cast-on can be used; for photo tutorials, see page 7.
• See page 17 for a photo tutorial on Russian Bind-Off.

Left Front

Row 1: Work Row 1 of Chart B, working patt rep 10 (11, 12) times.

Continue to work in patt through all 28 rows of Chart B until Left Front measures 19^1/$_2$ (20^1/$_2$, 21^1/$_4$) in./49.5 (52, 54) cm.

Next row: Sl wyif, k to end.

Rep last row 5 more times (6 rows in total).

BO using Russian Bind-Off.

Right Back

Undo provisional cast-on from Left Back and place sts on a needle, ready to work a RS row—106 (116, 126) sts.

Complete as for Left Back until Right Back matches Left Back to armhole bind off, ending with a WS row.

Next row (RS): Sl wyif, k36 (42, 48), RBO 40 (42, 44), k to end.

Next row (WS): Sl wyif, k2, p26 (28, 30), Cable Cast-On 40 (42, 44), p to last 3 sts, k3.

Right Front

Complete as for Left Front.

Left Back

Using any provisional cast-on method, CO 107 (117, 127) sts.

Set-up row: Purl all sts, purling 2 tog in the middle of the row to dec extra provisional cast-on st—106 (116, 126) sts.

Row 1 (RS): Work Row 1 of Chart A, working patt rep 50 (55, 60) times.

Continue to work in patt through all 10 rows of Chart A until Left Back measures 7 in./18 cm (8 in./20.5 cm, 8^3/$_4$ in./22 cm), ending with a WS row.

Next row (RS): Sl wyif, k28 (30, 32), RBO 40, (42, 44) sts, k to end.

Next row (WS): Sl wyif, k2, p34 (40, 46), Cable Cast-On 40 (42, 44) sts, p to last 3 sts, k3—106, (116, 126) sts.

Finishing

Weave in loose ends. Block vest.

Chart A

Pattern repeat is in [ ].

Rows 1, 3, and 9 (RS): Sl wyif, k to end.
Rows 2, 8, and 10 (WS): Sl wyif, k2, p to last 3 sts, k3.
Rows 4 and 6: Sl wyif, k to end.
Row 5: Sl wyif, k2, [k2tog, yo] to last 3 sts, k3.
Row 7: Sl wyif, k2, [k1, k1tbl] to last 3 sts, k3.

Chart B

Pattern repeat is in [ ].

Rows 1, 3, 7, 11, 15, 17, 21, and 25 (RS): Sl wyif, k to end.
Row 2 and all WS rows: Sl wyif, k2, p to last 3 sts, k3.
Rows 5, 9, and 13: Sl wyif, k2, [(B, yo) 3 times, B, (ssk) 3 times], k3.
Rows 19, 23, and 27: Sl wyif, k2, [(k2tog) 3 times, (B, yo) 3 times, B], k3.

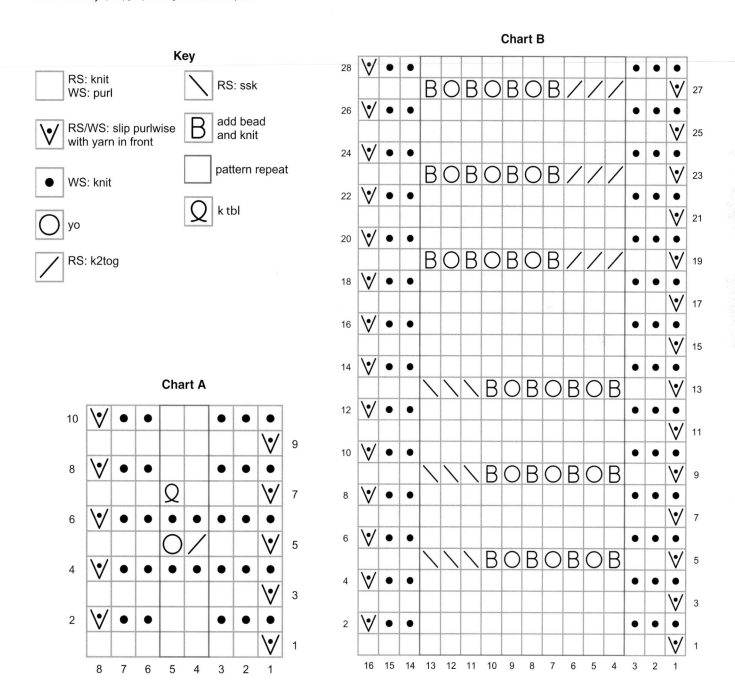

Key

☐ RS: knit / WS: purl	╲ RS: ssk
V RS/WS: slip purlwise with yarn in front	B add bead and knit
● WS: knit	☐ pattern repeat
○ yo	Ω k tbl
╱ RS: k2tog	

Chart A

Chart B

Lucinda

An all-over diamond lace pattern with little flower motifs and beads adorns this triangular shawl. It is perfect to wear around the shoulders or bunched up around your neck as a scarf.

FINISHED MEASUREMENTS
Width: 56 in./142 cm
Depth: 31^1/$_2$ in./80 cm

YARN
Cascade Yarns Heritage 150 Sock Yarn, fingering weight #1 yarn, 75% superwash merino wool/25% nylon, 492 yd./450 m, 5.25 oz./150 g
• 2 skeins #5605

NEEDLES AND OTHER MATERIALS
• US 6 (4 mm) circular needle, 32 in./80 cm long
• 544 lavender size 6 seed beads (debbieabrahamsbeads.co.uk, #337 Lavender)
• US 13 (0.75 mm) steel crochet hook (for adding beads)
• Removable stitch marker (optional)
• Tapestry needle

GAUGE
23 sts x 26.5 rows in Chart B patt after blocking = 4 in./10 cm square
Be sure to check your gauge!

Skill Level
Level 1

Notes

• The shawl is worked in rows on a circular needle from the bottom up, with decreases worked on every other row to shape it.
• Cast on using a stretchy cast-on like long-tail holding two needles together.
• In the directions, the stitch in bold is the "center spine" of the shawl. You may wish to place a lockable marker on this stitch to help you keep track of the pattern.
• Charts show only RS rows. See pattern for WS rows.

Cast On

CO 323 sts.
Knit one row.

Work Chart A

Row 1 (RS): Sl wyif, k1, work Row 1 of Chart A working patt rep 10 times, **k1**, work Row 1 of Chart A working patt rep 10 times, k2—4 sts dec'd.

Row 2 and all WS rows: Sl wyif, k1, p to last 2 sts, k2.

Row 3: Sl wyif, k1, work Row 3 of Chart A working patt rep 10 times, **k1**, work Row 3 of Chart A working patt rep 10 times, k2—4 sts dec'd.

Continue to work in patt through all 12 rows of Chart A once—299 sts.

Work Chart B

Row 1 (RS): Sl wyif, k1, work Row 1 of Chart B working patt rep 9 times, **k1**, work Row 1 of Chart B working patt rep 9 times, k2—4 sts dec'd.

Row 2 and all WS rows: Sl wyif, k1, p to last 2 sts, k2.

Row 3: Sl wyif, k1, work Row 3 of Chart B working patt rep 9 times, **k1**, work Row 3 of Chart B working patt rep 9 times, k2—4 sts dec'd.

Continue to work in patt through all 24 rows of Chart B for a total of 4 times, working one less patt rep on each half of the shawl for each repeat of the Chart—107 sts.

Finish Shawl

Row 1 (RS): Sl wyif, k1, ssk, k47, k2tog, **k1**, ssk, k47, k2tog, k2—4 sts dec'd.

Row 2 and all WS rows: Sl wyif, k1, p to last 2 sts, k2.

Row 3: Sl wyif, k1, ssk, k45, k2tog, **k1**, ssk, k45, k2tog, k2—4 sts dec'd.

Row 5: Sl wyif, k1, ssk, k43, k2tog, **k1**, ssk, k43, k2tog, k2—4 sts dec'd.

Continue to decrease in patt until 11 sts rem.

Next RS row: Sl wyif, k1, sl1, k2tog, psso, **k1**, sl1, k2tog, psso, k2—4 sts dec'd.

Next RS row: Sl wyif, k1, sl1, k2tog, psso, k2—2 sts dec'd, 5 sts.

BO rem sts.

Finishing

Weave in loose ends. Block shawl.

Chart A

Pattern repeat is in [ ].

Row 1 (RS): Ssk, k5, k2tog, k4, B, yo, B, k4, [k2tog, k4, B, yo, B, k4], k2tog, k4, B, yo, B, k10, k2tog.

Row 3: Ssk, k4, k2tog, k3, B, yo, k1, yo, B, k3, [sl1, k2tog, psso, k3, B, yo, k1, yo, B, k3], sl1, k2tog, psso, k3, B, yo, k1, yo, B, k3, ssk, k4, k2tog.

Row 5: Ssk, k3, k2tog, k2, B, yo, k3, yo, B, k2, [sl1, k2tog, psso, k2, B, yo, k3, yo, B, k2], sl1, k2tog, psso, k2, B, yo, k3, yo, B, k2, ssk, k3, k2tog.

Row 7: Ssk, k2, k2tog, k1, B, yo, k2tog, yo, k1, yo, ssk, yo, B, k1, [sl1, k2tog, psso, k1, B, yo, k2tog, yo, k1, yo, ssk, yo, B, k1], sl1, k2tog, psso, k1, B, yo, k2tog, yo, k1, yo, ssk, yo, B, k1, ssk, k2, k2tog.

Row 9: Ssk, k1, k2tog, B, yo, k2tog, yo, k3, yo, ssk, yo, B, [sl1, k2tog, psso, B, yo, k2tog, yo, k3, yo, ssk, yo, B], sl1, k2tog, psso, B, yo, k2tog, yo, k3, yo, ssk, yo, B, ssk, k1, k2tog.

Row 11: Ssk, (k2tog, yo) 3 times, k1, (yo, ssk) 2 times, yo, [sl1, k2tog, psso, (yo, k2tog) 2 times, yo, k1, (yo, ssk) 2 times, yo], sl1, k2tog, psso, (yo, k2tog) 2 times, yo, k1, (yo, ssk,) 3 times, k2tog.

Chart B

Pattern repeat is in [ ].

Row 1: Ssk, k10, k2tog, yo, k5, [k5, k2tog, yo, k5], k5, k2tog, yo, k11, k2tog.

Row 3: Ssk, k4, B, k3, k2tog, yo, k1, yo, ssk, k3, [B, k3, k2tog, yo, k1, yo, ssk, k3], B, k3, k2tog, yo, k1, yo, ssk, k3, B, k4, k2tog.

Row 5: Ssk, k2, (B, k1) 2 times, k2tog, yo, k3, yo, ssk, k1, B, [k1, B, k1, k2tog, yo, k3, yo, ssk, k1, B], k1, B, k1, k2tog, yo, k3, yo, ssk, (k1, B) 2 times, k2, k2tog.

Row 7: Ssk, k2, B, k1, (k2tog, yo) 2 times, k1, (yo, ssk) 2 times, k1, [B, k1, (k2tog, yo) 2 times, k1, (yo, ssk) 2 times, k1], B, k1, (k2tog, yo) 2 times, k1, (yo, ssk) 2 times, k1, B, k2, k2tog.

Row 9: Ssk, k2, (k2tog, yo) 2 times, k3, (yo, ssk) 2 times, [k1, (k2tog, yo) 2 times, k3, (yo, ssk) 2 times], k1, (k2tog, yo) 2 times, k3, (yo, ssk) 2 times, k2, k2tog.

Row 11: Ssk, k2tog, yo, k3, yo, sl1, k2tog, psso, yo, k3, yo, [(sl1, k2tog, psso, yo, k3, yo) 2 times], (sl1, k2tog, psso, yo, k3, yo) 2 times, ssk, k2tog.

Row 13: Ssk, k10, k2tog, [yo, k10, k2tog], yo, k11, k2tog.

Row 15: Ssk, k4, B, k3, k2tog, yo, [k1, yo, ssk, k3, B, k3, k2tog, yo], k1, yo, ssk, k3, B, k4, k2tog.

Row 17: Ssk, k2, (B, k1) 2 times, k2tog, yo, k1, [k2, yo, ssk, (k1, B) 2 times, k1, k2tog, yo, k1], k2, yo, ssk, (k1, B) 2 times, k2, k2tog.

Row 19: Ssk, k2, B, k1, (k2tog, yo) 2 times, [k1, (yo, ssk) 2 times, k1, B, k1, (k2tog, yo) 2 times], k1, (yo, ssk) 2 times, k1, B, k2, k2tog.

Row 21: Ssk, k2, (k2tog, yo) 2 times, k1, [k2, (yo, ssk) 2 times, k1, (k2tog, yo) 2 times, k1], k2, (yo, ssk) 2 times, k2, k2tog.

Row 23: Ssk, k2tog, yo, k3, yo, [(sl1, k2tog, psso, yo, k3, yo) 2 times], sl1, k2tog, psso, yo, k3, yo, ssk, k2tog.

Key

knit

ssk

k2tog

yo

sl1, k2tog, psso

B — add bead and knit

pattern repeat

Chart A

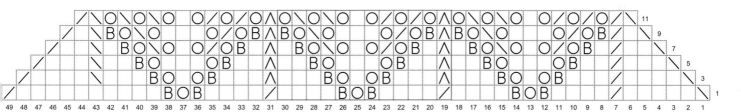

Chart B

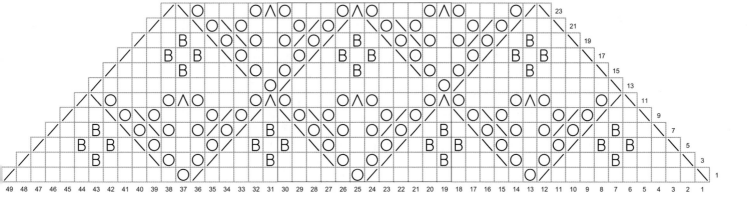

Adelaide

I n Adelaide a beautiful lace pattern, beads, and luxurious hand-dyed yarn combine to create a truly stunning accessory.

FINISHED MEASUREMENTS
Width: 19 in./48 cm
Length: 89 in./226 cm

YARN
Fyberspates Gleem Lace, lace weight #0 yarn, 55% super-wash British Bluefaced Leicester wool/45% silk, 874 yd./800 m, 3.5 oz./100 g
• 1 skein #710 Lavender Haze

NEEDLES AND OTHER MATERIALS
• US 4 (3.5 mm) straight or circular needles, any length
• 2,356 lavender size 6 seed beads
  (debbieabrahamsbeads.co.uk, #337 Lavender)
• US 13 (0.75 mm) steel crochet hook (for adding beads)
• Tapestry needle

GAUGE
21 sts x 27 rows in Chart patt after blocking = 4 in./10 cm square
Be sure to check your gauge!

Skill Level
Level 2

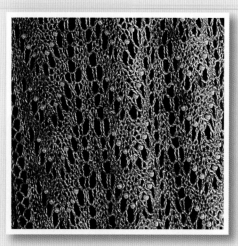

Notes

• If you prefer a shorter shawl, work fewer repeats of the chart.
• Do not work "k tbl" on Row 1 of first pattern repeat in chart.
• See page 17 for a photo tutorial of Russian Bind-Off.

Cast On and Garter Stitch Border

CO 77 sts.
Rows 1–6: K to end.

Center Panel

Row 1 (RS): Work Row 1 of Chart, working patt repeat 3 times.
Continue to work in patt through all 16 rows of Chart for a total of 38 times (608 rows).

Second Garter Stitch Border

Rows 1–6: K to end.
BO using Russian Bind-Off.

Finishing

Weave in loose ends. Block shawl.

Chart

Pattern repeat is in [ ].
Row 1 (RS): Sl wyif, k3, ssk, [yo, k2, k2tog, yo, k1, yo, sl1, k2tog, psso, yo, k1, yo, ssk, k2, yo, sl1, k2tog, psso], yo, k1, k2tog, k1, yo, k3, yo, k2tog, k6, k tbl, B, k1, k tbl, k2, yo, B, k1.
Row 2 (WS): Sl wyif, k1, p13, k2, yo, k2tog, p to last 4 sts, k4.
Row 3: Sl wyif, k3, ssk, [k2, B, yo, k2tog, yo, k3, yo, ssk, yo, B, k2, sl1, k2tog, psso], k2, B, yo, k4, yo, k2tog, k2, k2tog, (yo) 2 times, ssk, B, k1, B, k2tog, (yo) 2 times, ssk, yo, B, k1.
Row 4: Sl wyif, k1, p3, p tbl, p6, p tbl, p3, k2, yo, k2tog, p to last 4 sts, k4.
Row 5: Sl wyif, k3, ssk, [k1, B, yo, k2, yo, k2tog, k1, ssk, yo, k2, yo, B, k1, sl1, k2tog, psso], k1, B, yo, k5, yo, k2tog, k4, k tbl, B, k3, B, k1, k tbl, k2, yo, B, k1.
Row 6: Sl wyif, k1, p15, k2, yo, k2tog, p to last 4 sts, k4.
Row 7: Sl wyif, k3, ssk, [B, yo, k3, yo, k2tog, k1, ssk, yo, k3, yo, B, sl1, k2tog, psso], B, yo, k6, yo, (k2tog) 2 times , (yo) 2 times, ssk, B, k5, B, k2tog, (yo) 2 times, ssk, yo, B, k1.
Row 8: Sl wyif, k1, p3, p tbl, p10, p tbl, p1, k2, yo, k2tog, p to last 4 sts, k4.
Row 9: Sl wyif, k3, ssk, [yo, k2, k2tog, yo, k1, yo, sl1, k2tog, psso, yo, k1, yo, ssk, k2, yo, sl1, k2tog, psso], yo, k2, k2tog, yo, k3, yo, k2tog, k2, k tbl, k2, (B, k3) 2 times, k2tog, yo, k2tog, k1.

Row 10: Sl wyif, B, p15, k2, yo, k2tog, p to last 4 sts, k4.

Row 11: Sl wyif, k3, ssk, [k2, B, yo, k2tog, yo, k3, yo, ssk, yo, B, k2, sl1, k2tog, psso], k2, B, yo, k4, yo, k2tog, k2, k2tog, (yo) 2 times, ssk, B, k1, B, k2tog, (yo) 2 times, sl1, k2tog, psso, yo, k2tog, k1.

Row 12: Sl wyif, B, p3, p tbl, p6, p tbl, p3, k2, yo, k2tog, p to last 4 sts, k4.

Row 13: Sl wyif, k3, ssk, [k1, B, yo, k2, yo, k2tog, k1, ssk, yo, k2, yo, B, k1, sl1, k2tog, psso], k1, B, yo, k5, yo, k2tog, k4, k tbl, k2, B, k3, k2tog, yo, k2tog, k1.

Row 14: Sl wyif, B, p13, k2, yo, k2tog, p to last 4 sts, k4.

Row 15: Sl wyif, k3, ssk, [B, yo, k3, yo, k2tog, k1, ssk, yo, k3, yo, B, sl1, k2tog, psso], B, yo, k6, yo, k2tog, k4, k2tog, ((yo) 2 times, sl1, k2tog, psso) 2 times, yo, k2tog, k1.

Row 16: Sl wyif, B, p3, p tbl, p2, p tbl, p5, k2, yo, k2tog, p to last 4 sts, k4.

Key

☐	RS: knit / WS: purl
\	RS: ssk
O	RS/WS: yo
/	RS/WS: k2tog
∧	RS: sl1, k2tog, psso
B	RS/WS: add bead and knit
V̇	RS/WS: slip purlwise with yarn in front
•	RS: purl / WS: knit
Ω	RS: k tbl / WS: p tbl
☐	pattern repeat

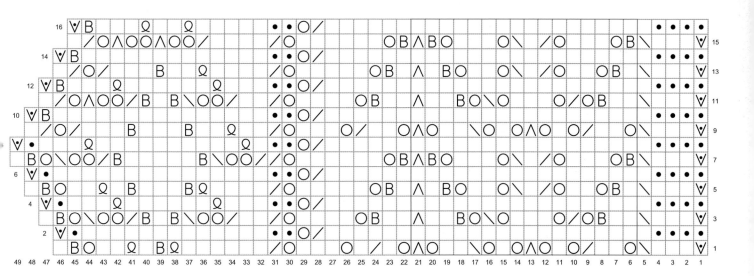

Edie

This scarf is worked as a long rectangle with a lacy center and a garter stitch edging. One end of the scarf will have buttonholes and the buttons will be used to create a long infinity loop which will enable the scarf to be worn wrapped around the neck twice. Alternatively, you can wear it as a single long loop or as a regular scarf. The buttons can be omitted if preferred. Simply knit the button row instead.

FINISHED MEASUREMENTS
Width: 13 in./33 cm
Length: 62 in./157.5 cm

YARN
Madelinetosh Merino Light, fingering weight #1 yarn, 100% superwash merino wool, 420 yd./384 m, 3.5 oz./100 g
• 2 skeins Fathom

NEEDLES AND OTHER MATERIALS
• US 6 (4 mm) straight or circular needles
• 2,080 mauve size 6 seed beads (debbieabrahamsbeads.co.uk, #227)
• US 13 (0.75 mm) steel crochet hook (for adding beads)
• 6 (3/4 in./2 cm) buttons
• Tapestry needle

GAUGE
21 sts x 27.5 rows in Chart patt after blocking = 4 in./10 cm square
Be sure to check your gauge!

SPECIAL STITCHES
Cable Cast-On: Insert RH needle between first 2 sts on LH needle, wrap yarn around needle and pull through to create a new st. Place new st on LH needle.

One-Row Buttonhole: Work to the place where you need to start the buttonhole.

1. Take the yarn to the front between the needles, slip one stitch purlwise to the right needle, take the yarn to the back between the needles.

2. *Slip the next stitch purlwise and pass the first slipped stitch over. Repeat from * until you have bound off the required number of stitches (or more if you prefer a larger buttonhole). Slip the stitch remaining on the right needle to the left needle and turn the work. The working yarn is now at the beginning of the left needle.

(continued)

Level 2

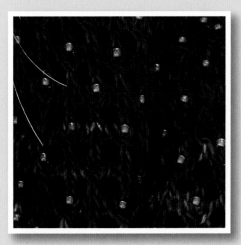

Notes

• The stitch highlighted in purple in the chart is worked as k2tog the very first time that stitch is worked on the chart, then every following time it's worked as a sl1, k2tog, psso.
• See page 17 for a photo tutorial for Russian Bind-Off.

3. With yarn at the back, Cable Cast-On the number of stitches you bound off plus one stitch (if you bound off 3, then cast on 4). Before placing the last stitch on the left needle, bring the yarn to the front between the needles, place the stitch on the left needle, and turn the work.

4. Slip the first stitch on the left needle knitwise, pass the last cast-on stitch over it, and tighten the stitch. The buttonhole is now complete and the total stitch count has not been altered.

Scarf

CO 69 sts.
Row 1 (RS): Sl wyif, k to end.
Row 2 (WS): Sl wyif, k to end.
Rep Rows 1–2 once more.
Next row (RS): Work Row 1 of Chart, working patt rep 3 times.
Next row (WS): Work Row 2 of Chart.
Continue working in patt through all 16 rows of Chart 26 times.
Next row (RS): Sl wyif, k to end.
Next row (WS): Sl wyif, k to end.
Rep last 2 rows once more.
Next row: K5, [work 3-st One-Row Buttonhole, k7] 5 times, work 3-st One-Row Buttonhole, k5.
Next row: Sl wyif, k to end.
Next row: Sl wyif, k to end.
BO using Russian Bind-Off.

Finishing

Weave in all loose ends. Block scarf. When dry, stitch buttons in place.

Chart

Pattern repeat is in [ ].
Row 1 (RS): Sl wyif, k3, k2tog, yo, k1, yo, sl1, k2tog, psso, yo, k2tog, yo, k1, yo, sl1, k2tog, psso, yo, k1, yo, ssk, yo, sl1, k2tog, psso, yo, k1, yo, [sl1, k2tog, psso, yo, k1, yo, sl1, k2tog, psso, yo, k2tog, yo, k1, yo, sl1, k2tog, psso, yo, k1, yo, ssk, yo, sl1, k2tog, psso, yo, k1, yo], ssk, k4.
Row 2 and all WS rows: Sl wyif, k3, p to last 4 sts, k4.
Row 3: Sl wyif, k3, [k2, B, k2, k2tog, yo, k2, yo, sl1, k2tog, psso, yo, k2, yo, ssk, k2, B, k1], k5.
Row 5: Sl wyif, k3, [k1, yo, sl1, k2tog, psso, yo, k1, yo, ssk, B, k5, B, k2tog, yo, k1, yo, sl1, k2tog, psso, yo], k5.
Row 7: Sl wyif, k3, [k4, B, k1, yo, ssk, B, k3, B, k2tog, yo, k1, B, k3], k5.
Row 9: Sl wyif, k3, k2tog, yo, k1, yo, sl1, k2tog, psso, yo, k1, yo, ssk, B, k1, B, k2tog, yo, k1, yo, sl1, k2tog, psso, yo, k1, yo, [(sl1, k2tog, psso, yo, k1, yo) 2 times, ssk, B, k1, B, k2tog, yo, k1, yo, sl1, k2tog, psso, yo, k1, yo], ssk, k4.
Row 11: Sl wyif, k3, [k2, B, k3, B, k1, yo, ssk, B, k2tog, yo, k1, B, k3, B, k1], k5.
Row 13: Sl wyif, k3, [(k1, yo, sl1, k2tog, psso, yo) 5 times], k5.
Row 15: Sl wyif, k3, [(B, k3) 5 times], k5.
Row 16: Sl wyif, k3, p to last 4 sts, k4.

Key

▨	work as k2tog in first pattern repeat
☐	RS: knit / WS: purl
O	RS: yo
/	RS: k2tog
\	RS: ssk
∧	RS: sl1, k2tog, psso
B	add bead and knit
☐	pattern repeat
V	RS/WS: slip purlwise with yarn in front
●	WS: knit

Christine

A beautiful bolero with a beaded lace pattern, Christine is elegant and perfect to wear over a little black dress to a party or a summer dress on a chilly summer evening.

Skill Level

Level 2

Notes

- The bolero is worked from the bottom up in three pieces, with stitches increased for the sleeves. A 2x2 rib is followed by an all-over beaded lace pattern.
- Chart shows only RS rows. See pattern for WS rows.
- For photo tutorials for Short-Row Shaping, Three-Needle Bind-Off, and Russian Bind-Off, see pages 22, 18, and 17, respectively.

FINISHED MEASUREMENTS

Small (Medium, Large)
Actual bust: $35^{1}/_{2}$ (44, 48) in./90 (112, 122) cm
Length: $13^{1}/_{2}$ ($14^{3}/_{4}$, 15) in./34.5 (37.5, 38) cm
Sleeve length to underarm: 4 ($4^{1}/_{4}$, $6^{1}/_{4}$) in./10 (11, 16) cm

YARN

Debbie Bliss Angel, lace weight #0 yarn, 76% super kid mohair/24% silk, 218 yd./200 m, 1 oz./25 g
- 4 (6, 7) balls #27 Teal

NEEDLES AND OTHER MATERIALS

- US 5 (3.75 mm) knitting needles
- US 5 (3.75 mm) circular needles, 16 in./40 cm long and 32 in./80 cm long
- 1,080 (1,260, 1,440) lime green size 6 seed beads (debbieabrahamsbeads.co.uk, #48 Lime)
- US 15 (0.50 mm) steel crochet hook (for adding beads)
- 5 ($^{3}/_{4}$ in./2 cm) buttons
- Stitch markers
- Stitch holder
- Tapestry needle

GAUGE

19 sts x 30 rows in Chart patt after blocking = 4 in./10 cm square
Be sure to check your gauge!

SPECIAL STITCHES

One-Row Buttonhole: Work to the place where you need to start the buttonhole.

1. Take the yarn to the front between the needles, slip one stitch purlwise to the right needle, take the yarn to the back between the needles.
2. *Slip the next stitch purlwise and pass the first slipped stitch over. Repeat from * until you have bound off the required number of stitches (or more if you prefer a larger buttonhole). Slip the stitch remaining on the right needle to the left needle and turn the work. The working yarn is now at the beginning of the left needle.

3. With yarn at the back, Cable Cast-On the number of stitches you bound off plus one stitch (if you bound off 3, then cast on 4). Before placing the last stitch on the left needle, bring the yarn to the front between the needles, place the stitch on the left needle, and turn the work.

4. Slip the first stitch on the left needle knitwise, pass the last cast-on stitch over it, and tighten the stitch. The buttonhole is now complete and the total stitch count has not been altered.

Cable Cast-On: Insert RH needle between first 2 sts on LH needle, wrap yarn around needle and pull through to create a new st. Place new st on LH needle.

Knitted Cast-On: Make a slip knot and place on needle. Hold needle in left hand, insert RH needle into stitch created by slip knot, and knit up a stitch as normal but leave the original loop on LH needle and place new stitch on LH needle. You will now have 2 sts.

Back

With straight needles, CO 86 (98, 114) sts.
Row 1 (RS): K2, *p2, k2, rep from * to end.
Row 2 (WS): P2, *k2, p2, rep from * to end.
Rep Rows 1 and 2 until ribbing measures 4 in./10 cm, ending with a WS row.

Small and Large Sizes Only
Next row (RS): K14 (19), m1, (k29 (38), m1) 2 times, k14 (19)—89 (117) sts.

Medium Size Only
Next row: K10, m1, (k19, m1, k20, m1) 2 times, k10—103 sts.

All Sizes
Next row: P to end.
Next row (RS): Work Row 1 of Chart, working patt rep 6 (7, 8) times.
Next row and all following WS rows: P to end.
Continue working in patt through all 36 rows of Back chart until the back measures 6 in./15.25 cm (6¼ in./15.75 cm, 6 in./15.25 cm).
Next row: P to end.

Add Sleeves
Next row (RS): Using Cable or Knitted Cast-On, CO 14 (21, 28) sts, work next row of chart as established—103 (124, 145) sts.
Next row (WS): Using Cable or Knitted Cast-On, CO 14 (21, 28) sts, p to end—117 (145, 173) sts.

Continue to work Chart as established until back measures 13¼ in./ 33.5 cm (14½ in./37 cm, 14¾ in./37.5 cm), ending with a WS row.

Shape Right Neck
Next row (RS): Work in patt for 43 (56, 69) sts, turn. Transfer rem sts to stitch holder.
Next row (WS): P1, p2tog, p to end—1 st dec'd.
Next row: Work in patt to last 3 sts, k2tog, k1—1 st dec, 41, (54, 67) sts.

Shape Right Shoulder
Next row (WS): P20 (26, 32), w&t.
Next row (RS): Work in patt to end.
Next row: P10 (13, 16), w&t.
Next row: Work in patt to end.
Next row: P to end, including wraps as they appear.
Put sts on holder.

Shape Left Neck
Leave center 31 (33, 35) sts on holder for back neck. Reattach yarn at neck edge and work in patt to end—43, (56, 69) sts.
Next row (WS): P to last 3 sts, p2tog tbl, p1—1 st dec'd.
Next row (RS): K1, ssk, work in patt to end—1 st dec'd, 41 (54, 67) sts.
Next row: P to end.

Shape Left Shoulder
Next row (RS): Work in patt 20 (26, 32) sts, w&t.
Next row (WS): P to end.
Next row: Work in patt 10 (13, 16) sts, w&t.
Next row: P to end.
Next row: Work in patt to end, including wraps as they appear.
Put sts on holder.

Left Front

Using straight needles, CO 42 (46, 54) sts.
Row 1 (RS): K2, *p2, k2, rep from * to end.
Row 2 (WS): P2, *k2, p2, rep from * to end.
Rep Rows 1 and 2 until ribbing measures same as for back, ending with a WS row.

Small and Medium Sizes Only
Next row: K7 (8), m1, (k14 (15), m1) 2 times, k7 (8)—45, (49) sts.
Next row: P to end.

Large Size Only
Next row: K5, m1, (k11, m1) 4 times, k5—59 sts.
Next row: P to end.

Medium Size Only
Next row: K2, work Row 1 of Chart, working patt rep 3 times, to last 2 sts of row, k2.
Next row: P to end.

Small and Large Sizes
Next row (RS): Work Row 1 of Chart, working patt rep 3 (4) times.
Next row and and all following WS rows: P to end.

All Sizes
Continue working through all 36 rows of Chart until the Left Front matches the Back to Add Sleeves, ending with a WS row.

Add Sleeves

Next row (RS): Using Cable or Knitted Cast-On, CO 14 (24, 28) sts, work next row of Chart as established—59, (73, 87) sts.
Next Row 2 and all following WS rows: P to end.
Continue in patt as established until Left Front measures 8³/₄ (9¹/₂, 9¹/₂) in./22 (24, 24) cm, ending with a WS row.

Shape Neck

Row 1 (RS): Work in patt to last 3 sts, k2tog, k1—1 st dec'd.

Row 2 and all following WS rows: P1, p2tog, p to end—1 st dec'd.

Rep [Rows 1 and 2] 8 (8, 9) more times.

Rep [Row 1] 0 (1, 0) more times—41(54, 67) sts.

Shape Shoulder

Row 1 (WS): P20 (26, 32), w&t.

Row 2 (RS): Work in patt to end.

Row 3: P10 (13, 16), w&t.

Row 4: Work in patt to end.

Row 5: P to end, including wraps as they appear.

Put sts on holder.

Right Front

Complete as for Left Front up to Add Sleeves.

Add Sleeves

Next row (WS): Using Cable or Knitted Cast-On, CO 14, (24, 28) sts, p to end—59, (73, 87) sts.

Next row (RS): Work in patt to end.

Continue in patt as established until Right Front matches Left Front to neck shaping, ending with a WS row.

Shape Neck

Row 1 (RS): K1, ssk, work in patt to end—1 st dec'd.

Row 2 (WS): P to last 3 sts, p2tog tbl, p1—1 st dec'd.

Rep [Rows 1 and 2] 8 (8, 9) more times.

Rep [Row 1] 0, (1, 0) more times—41, (54, 67) sts.

Shape Shoulder

Row 1 (RS): Work in patt 20, (26, 32) sts, w&t.

Row 2 (WS): P to end.

Row 3: Work in patt 10 (13, 16) sts, w&t.

Row 4: P to end.

Row 5: Work in patt to end including wraps as they appear.

Put sts on holder.

Finishing

Block pieces to measurements. Join shoulder seams with a Three-Needle Bind-Off with WS of pieces facing. Seam underarm and side seams.

Sleeve Edging

Using the 16 in./40 cm circular needle and starting at the underarm with RS facing, pick up and k80 (88, 92) sts around sleeve. Join to work in the round. Place a st marker to mark beg of round.

Rnd 1: P.

Rnd 2: K.

Rnd 3: P.

BO using Russian Bind-Off.

Button Band

Using the longer circular needle and starting at the lower Right Front with RS facing, pick up and k50 (54, 56) sts to right neck, pick up and k30 (35, 36) sts to right shoulder, pick up and k5 sts to back neck, k31 (33, 35) sts along back neck, pick up and k5 sts to left shoulder, pick up and k30 (35, 36) sts along left neck, pick up and k51 (55, 57) sts along left front—202 (222, 230) sts.

Row 1 (WS): *P2, k2, rep from * to last 2 sts, p2.

Row 2 (RS): *K2, p2, rep from * to last 2 sts, k2.

Rows 3 and 4: Rep Rows 1 and 2.

Row 5: *P2, k2, rep from * to last 2 sts, p2.

Row 6: Work in rib as set 4 (4, 5) sts, [work 4-st One-Row Buttonhole, work in rib as set 5 (6, 6) sts] 4 times, work 4-st One-Row Buttonhole, continue in patt to end.

Rows 7 and 8: Rep Rows 1 and 2.

BO loosely in patt.

Sew on buttons. Weave in loose ends.

Chart

Pattern repeat is in [ ].

Stitches in boldface work only on Back of bolero.

**In final patt repeat, substitute this sl1, k2tog, psso with ssk.

Row 1 (RS): K1, k2, [k4, yo, ssk, k1, k2tog, yo, k5], k1, **k1**.

Row 2 and all WS rows: P to end.

Row 3: K1, k2, [k2, k2tog, yo, B, yo, sl1, k2tog, psso, yo, B, yo, ssk, k3], k1, **k1**.

Row 5: K1, k2, [k1, k2tog, yo, B, k1, yo, sl1, k2tog, psso, yo, k1, B, yo, ssk, k2], k1, **k1**.

Row 7: K1, k2, [k2tog, yo, B, k2, yo, sl1, k2tog, psso, yo, k2, B, yo, ssk, k1], k1, **k1**.

Row 9: K1, k1, k2tog, [yo, B, k3, yo, sl1, k2tog, psso, yo, k3, B, yo, sl1, k2tog, psso**], k1, **k1**.

Row 11: K1, k1, k2tog, [(yo, k4, yo, sl1, k2tog, psso**) 2 times], k1, **k1**.

Row 13: K1, k1, k2tog, [yo, k2, k2tog, yo, B, k1, B, yo, ssk, k2, yo, sl1, k2tog, psso**], k1, **k1**.

Row 15: K1, k1, k2tog, [yo, k1, k2tog, yo, B, k3, B, yo, ssk, k1, yo, sl1, k2tog, psso**], k1, **k1**.

Row 17: K1, k1, k2tog, [yo, k2tog, yo, B, k5, B, yo, ssk, yo, sl1, k2tog, psso**], k1, **k1**.

(continued)

Row 19: K1, k2, [k2tog, yo, B, k7, B, yo, ssk, k1], k1, **k1.**

Row 21: K1, k1, k2tog, [yo, B, yo, ssk, k5, k2tog, yo, B, yo, sl1, k2tog, psso**], k1, **k1.**

Row 23: K1, k1, k2tog, [yo, k1, B, yo, ssk, k3, k2tog, yo, B, k1, yo, sl1, k2tog, psso**], k1, **k1.**

Row 25: K1, k1, k2tog, [yo, k2, B, yo, ssk, k1, k2tog, yo, B, k2, yo, sl1, k2tog, psso**], k1, **k1.**

Row 27: K1, k1, k2tog, [yo, k3, B, yo, sl1, k2tog, psso, yo, B, k3, yo, sl1, k2tog, psso**], k1, **k1.**

Row 29: K1, k1, k2tog, [(yo, k4, yo, sl1, k2tog, psso**) 2 times], k1, **k1.**

Row 31: K1, k2, [B, yo, ssk, k2, yo, sl1, k2tog, psso, yo, k2, k2tog, yo, B, k1], k1, **k1.**

Row 33: K1, k2, [k1, B, yo, ssk, k1, yo, sl1, k2tog, psso, yo, k1, k2tog, yo, B, k2], k1, **k1.**

Row 35: K1, k2, [k2, B, yo, ssk, yo, sl1, k2tog, psso, yo, k2tog, yo, B, k3], k1, **k1.**

Key

- only work on back
- work as ssk in last pattern repeat
- knit
- O yo
- / k2tog
- \ ssk
- ∧ sl1, k2tog, psso
- B add bead and knit
- pattern repeat

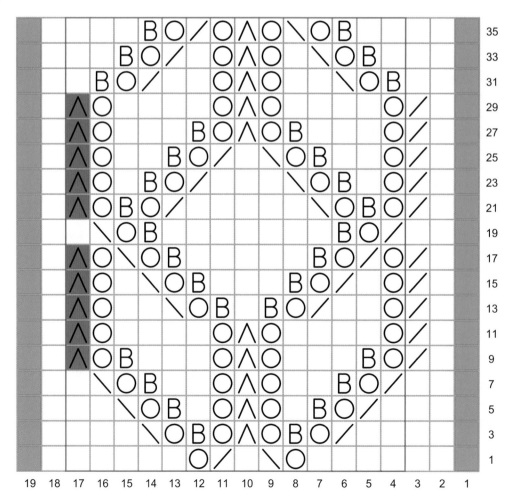

This square shawl is worked from the center out in the round. I recommend using double-pointed needles to start, then changing to various lengths of circular needles as required. But you can also cast on using a circular needle and the magic loop technique.

Skill Level

Level 2

Notes

- Emily Ocker's Circular Cast-On or Disappearing Loop Cast-On is recommended but other circular cast-ons can be used if preferred; see pages 13–17 for photo tutorials.
- For a photo tutorial for Russian Bind-Off, see page 17.

FINISHED MEASUREMENTS
Each side: 56 in./142 cm

YARN
Fyberspates Scrumptious Lace, lace weight #0 yarn, 55% merino wool/45% silk, 1,093 yd./1,000 m, 3.5 oz./100 g
- 2 skeins #508 Midnight

NEEDLES AND OTHER MATERIALS
- US 4 (3.5 mm) set of double-pointed needles
- US 4 (3.5 mm) circular needles, 16 in./40 cm and 32 in./80 cm long
- 2,212 light blue size 8 seed beads (debbieabrahamsbeads.co.uk, #387 Baby Blue)
- US 15 (0.50 mm) steel crochet hook (for adding beads)
- Stitch marker
- Tapestry needle

GAUGE
31 sts x 16 rows in Chart C patt after blocking = 4 in./10 cm square
Be sure to check your gauge!

Cast On

Using dpns, CO 8 sts. Divide sts evenly between 4 needles, being careful not to twist them. Join to work in the rnd. Place a marker to mark beg of rnd.
Knit one rnd.

Work Chart A

Rnd 1: (Work Rnd 1 of Chart A, k1) 4 times—8 sts inc'd.
Rnd 2 and all even-numbered rnds: K to end.
Continue to work in patt through all 22 rnds of Chart A once—96 sts.

Work Chart B

Rnd 1: (Work Rnd 1 of Chart B, working patt rep once, k1) 4 times—8 sts inc'd.
Rnd 2 and all even-numbered rnds: K to end.
Continue to work in patt through all 12 rnds of Chart B a total of 8 times. Each time you rep Chart B, work the patt

rep an additional time (for the second time around on the chart, work patt rep 2 times, etc.)—480 sts.

Work Chart C

Rnd 1: (Work Rnd 1 of Chart C, working patt rep 9 times, k1) 4 times—8 sts inc'd.
Rnd 2 and all even-numbered rnds: K to end.
Continue to work in patt through all 12 rnds of Chart C a total of 8 times. Each time you rep Chart C, work patt rep an additional time (for the second time around on the chart, work patt rep 10 times, etc.)—864 sts.

Work Chart D

Rnd 1: (Work Rnd 1 of Chart D, working patt rep 17 times, k1) 4 times—8 sts inc'd.
Rnd 2 and all even-numbered rnds: K to end.
Continue to work in patt through all 12 rnds of Chart D once—912 sts.
BO using Russian Bind-Off.

Finishing

Weave in loose ends. Block shawl.

Chart A

Rnd 1: Yo, k1, yo.
Rnd 2 and all even-numbered rnds: K to end.
Rnd 3: Yo, k3, yo.
Rnd 5: Yo, k5, yo.
Rnd 7: Yo, k7, yo.
Rnd 9: Yo, k9, yo.
Rnd 11: Yo, k3, k2tog, yo, k1, yo, ssk, k3, yo.
Rnd 13: Yo, k3, k2tog, yo, k3, yo, ssk, k3, yo.
Rnd 15: Yo, k3, k2tog, yo, k5, yo, ssk, k3, yo.
Rnd 17: Yo, k4, yo, sl1, k2tog, psso, yo, k3, yo, sl1, k2tog, yo, k4, yo.
Rnd 19: Yo, k19, yo.
Rnd 21: Yo, k21, yo.

Chart B

Pattern repeat is in [ ].

Rnd 1: Yo, k6, [k3, k2tog, yo, k1, yo, ssk, k4], k5, yo.
Rnd 2 and all even-numbered rnds: K to end.
Rnd 3: Yo, k2, yo, ssk, k3, [k2, k2tog, yo, k3, yo, ssk, k3], k2, k2tog, yo, k2, yo.
Rnd 5: Yo, k4, yo, ssk, k2, [k1, k2tog, yo, k5, yo, ssk, k2], k1, k2tog, yo, k4, yo.
Rnd 7: Yo, k4, yo, sl1, k2tog, psso, yo, k2, [k1, yo, sl1, k2tog, psso, yo, k3, yo, sl1, k2tog, psso, yo, k2], k1, yo, sl1, k2tog, psso, yo, k4, yo.
Rnd 9: Yo, k10, [k12], k9, yo.
Rnd 11: Yo, k11, [k12], k10, yo.

Chart C

Pattern repeat is in [ ].

Rnd 1: Yo, k6, [k3, k2tog, yo, k1, yo, ssk, k4], k5, yo.
Rnd 2 and all even-numbered rnds: K to end.

Key

- ☐ knit
- ◯ yo
- ╱ k2tog
- ╲ ssk
- ⋀ sl1, k2tog, psso
- B add bead and knit
- ☐ pattern repeat

Chart A

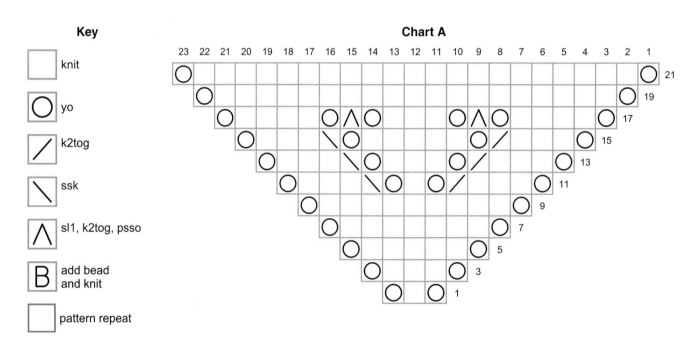

Chart B

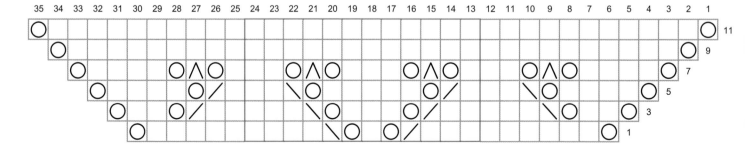

Rnd 3: Yo, k2, yo, ssk, k3, [k2, k2tog, yo, k3, yo, ssk, k3], k2, k2tog, yo, k2, yo.

Rnd 5: Yo, k1, B, k2, yo, ssk, k2, [k1, k2tog, yo, k2, B, k2, yo, ssk, k2], k1, k2tog, yo, k2, B, k1, yo.

Rnd 7: Yo, k3, B, k2, yo, ssk, k1, [k2tog, yo, k2, B, k1, B, k2, yo, ssk, k1], k2tog, yo, k2, B, k3, yo.

Rnd 9: Yo, k3, B, k1, k2tog, yo, k3, [k2, yo, ssk, k1, B, k1, k2tog, yo, k3], k2, yo, ssk, k1, B, k3, yo.

Rnd 11: Yo, k5, k2tog, yo, k4, [k3, yo, ssk, k1, k2tog, yo, k4], k3, yo, ssk, k5, yo.

Chart D

Pattern repeat is in [ ].

Rnd 1: Yo, k2, yo, ssk, yo, [sl1, k2tog, psso, (yo, k2tog) 2 times, yo, B, (yo, ssk) 2 times, yo], sl1, k2tog, psso, yo, k2tog, yo, k2, yo.

Rnd 2 and all even-numbered rnds: K to end.

Rnd 3: Yo, k2, (yo, ssk) 2 times, [B, (k2tog, yo) 2 times, k3, (yo, ssk) 2 times], B, (k2tog, yo) 2 times, k2, yo.

Rnd 5: Yo, k2, (yo, ssk) 2 times, yo, [sl1, k2tog, psso, (yo, k2tog) 2 times, yo, B, (yo, ssk) 2 times, yo], sl1, k2tog, psso, (yo, k2tog) 2 times, yo, k2, yo.

Rnd 7: Yo, k2, (yo, ssk) 3 times, [B, (k2tog, yo) 2 times, k3, (yo, ssk) 2 times], B, (k2tog, yo) 3 times, k2, yo.

Rnd 9: Yo, k4, (yo, ssk) 2 times, yo, [sl1, k2tog, psso, (yo, k2tog) 2 times, yo, B, (yo, ssk) 2 times, yo], sl1, k2tog, psso, (yo, k2tog) 2 times, yo, k4, yo.

Rnd 11: Yo, k6, (yo, ssk) 2 times, [B, (k2tog, yo) 2 times, k3, (yo, ssk) 2 times], B, (k2tog, yo) 2 times, k6, yo.

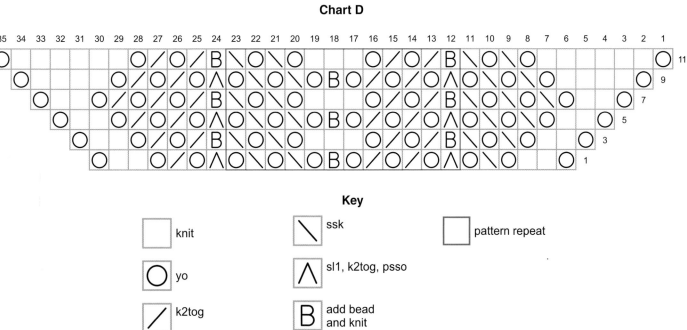

Chart C

Chart D

Key

knit

○ yo

╱ k2tog

╲ ssk

∧ sl1, k2tog, psso

B add bead and knit

pattern repeat

This shawl starts with the beaded lace section. The crescent shape is achieved by working a combination of short rows and decreases in garter stitch.

FINISHED MEASUREMENTS
Inner crescent: 61 in./155 cm
Outer crescent: 99^1/$_2$ in./253 cm
Depth: 21 in./53.5 cm

YARN
Manos del Uruguay Silk Blend Fino, fingering weight #1 yarn, 70% wool/30% silk, 246 yd./225 m, 1.75 oz./50 g
• 2 skeins #2600 Magenta

NEEDLES AND OTHER MATERIALS
• US 6 (4 mm) needles (32 in./80 cm circular needle recommended)
• 117 (4 mm) pink miracle beads
• US 13 (0.75 mm) steel crochet hook (for adding beads)
• Tapestry needle

GAUGE
13 sts x 15.5 rows in Chart B patt after blocking = 4 in./10 cm square
Be sure to check your gauge!

Skill Level
Level 2

Notes

• This shawl needs a stretchy cast-on. I recommend using the Long-Tail Cast-On holding two needles together. For a photo tutorial for Long-Tail Cast-On, see page 12.
• The charts include RS rows only. See pattern for WS rows.
• For a photo tutorial on Short-Row Shaping, see page 22.

Beaded Edge

CO 261 sts.
Row 1 (WS): K3, [k7, B, k15, B, k8] 8 times, k2.
Row 2 (RS): K to end.
Row 3: K to end.

Work Chart A

Row 1 (RS): Work Row 1 of Chart A, working patt repeat 8 times—2 sts inc'd.
Row 2 and all WS rows: K2, p to last 2 sts, k2.
Continue to work in patt through all 12 rows of Chart A once—273 sts.

Work Chart B

Row 1 (RS): Work Row 1 of Chart B, working patt repeat 8 times—2 sts inc'd.
Row 2 and all WS rows: K2, p to last 2 sts, k2.
Continue to work in patt through all 42 rows of Chart B once—315 sts.

Work Chart C

Row 1 (RS): Work Row 1 of Chart C, working patt repeat 8 times—2 sts inc'd.
Row 2 and all WS rows: K2, p to last 2 sts, k2.
Continue to work in patt through all 24 rows of Chart C once—325 sts.

Short-Row Section

Working in garter stitch short rows (without wrapping the sts), continue as follows:

Row 1 (RS): K169, turn—156 sts remain unworked.

Row 2 (WS): Sl wyif, k12, turn—156 sts remain unworked.

Next row: Sl wyif, k to 1 st before last turning point, ssk, k3, turn—1 st dec'd.

Next row: Sl wyif, k to 1 st before last turning point, ssk, k3, turn—1 st dec'd.

Rep last 2 rows until all remaining unworked sts have been worked—247 sts.

BO all sts.

Finishing

Weave in loose ends. Block shawl.

Chart A

Pattern repeat is in [ ].

Row 1 (RS): K2, yo, k1, [(yo, ssk, k11, k2tog, yo, k1) 2 times], yo, k2.

Row 2 and WS rows: K2, p to last 2 sts, k2.

Row 3: K2, yo, k2, [k1, yo, ssk, k9, k2tog, yo, k3, yo, ssk, k9, k2tog, yo, k2], k1, yo, k2.

Row 5: K2, yo, k3, [k2, yo, ssk, k7, k2tog, yo, k5, yo, ssk, k7, k2tog, yo, k3], k2, yo, k2.

Row 7: K2, yo, k2, yo, sl1, k2tog, psso, [(yo, k2, yo, ssk, k5, k2tog, yo, k2, yo, sl1, k2tog, psso) 2 times], yo, k2, yo, k2.

Row 9: K2, yo, k2, yo, ssk, B, [(k2tog, yo, k11, yo, ssk, B) 2 times], k2tog, yo, k2, yo, k2.

Row 11: K2, yo, k4, yo, sl1, k2tog, psso, [(yo, k13, yo, sl1, k2tog, psso) 2 times], yo, k4, yo, k2.

Chart B

Pattern repeat is in [ ].

Row 1 (RS): K2, yo, k7, [k5, k2tog, yo, k1, yo, ssk, k11, k2tog, yo, k1, yo, ssk, k6], k6, yo, k2.

Row 2 and all WS rows: K2, p to last 2 sts, k2.

Row 3: K2, yo, k1, yo, ssk, k5, [k4, k2tog, yo, k3, yo, ssk, k9, k2tog, yo, k3, yo, ssk, k5], k4, k2tog, yo, k1, yo, k2.

Row 5: K2, yo, k3, yo, ssk, k4, [k3, k2tog, yo, k5, yo, ssk, k7, k2tog, yo, k5, yo, ssk, k4], k3, k2tog, yo, k3, yo, k2.

Row 7: K2, yo, k5, yo, ssk, k3, [k2, k2tog, yo, k7, yo, ssk, k2tog, yo, k1, yo, ssk, k2tog, yo, k7, yo, ssk, k3], k2, k2tog, yo, k5, yo, k2.

Row 9: K2, yo, k2, B, k4, yo, ssk, k2, [k1, k2tog, yo, k4, B, k4, k2tog, yo, k3, yo, ssk, k4, B, k4, yo, ssk, k2], k1, k2tog, yo, k4, B, k2, yo, k2.

Row 11: K2, yo, k7, k2tog, yo, k3, [k2, yo, ssk, k7, k2tog, yo, k5, yo, ssk, k7, k2tog, yo, k3], k2, yo, ssk, k7, yo, k2.

Row 13: K2, yo, k3, k2tog, yo, k2, k2tog, yo, k4, [k3, yo, ssk, k1, k2tog, yo, k2, k2tog, yo, k7, yo, ssk, k1, k2tog, yo, k2, k2tog, yo, k4], k3, yo, ssk, k1, k2tog, yo, k4, yo, k2.

(continued)

Key

☐	knit	∧	sl1, k2tog, psso
O	yo	B	add bead and knit
\	ssk	☐	pattern repeat
/	k2tog		

Chart A

Row 15: K2, yo, k2, yo, sl1, k2tog, psso, yo, k1, yo, sl1, k2tog, psso, yo, k5, [k4, yo, sl1, k2tog, psso, yo, k1, yo, sl1, k2tog, psso, yo, k4, B, k4, yo, sl1, k2tog, psso, yo, k1, yo, sl1, k2tog, psso, yo, k5], k4, yo, sl1, k2tog, psso, yo, k1, yo, sl1, k2tog, psso, yo, k2, yo, k2.

Row 17: K2, yo, k15, [k10, yo, ssk, k7, k2tog, yo, k11], k14, yo, k2.

Row 19: K2, yo, k16, [k11, yo, ssk, k1, k2tog, yo, k2, k2tog, yo, k12], k15, yo, k2.

Row 21: K2, yo, k17, [k12, yo, sl1, k2tog, psso, yo, k1, yo, sl1, k2tog, psso, yo, k13], k16, yo, k2.

Row 23: K2, yo, k6, k2tog, (k1, yo) 2 times, k1, ssk, k5, [k4, k2tog, (k1, yo) 2 times, k1, ssk, k9, k2tog, (k1, yo) 2 times, k1, ssk, k5], k4, k2tog, (k1, yo) 2 times, k1, ssk, k6, yo, k2.

Row 25: K2, yo, k6, k2tog, k1, yo, k3, yo, k1, ssk, k4, [k3, k2tog, k1, yo, k3, yo, k1, ssk, k7, k2tog, k1, yo, k3, yo, k1, ssk, k4], k3, k2tog, k1, yo, k3, yo, k1, ssk, k6, yo, k2.

Row 27: K2, yo, k6, k2tog, k1, yo, k5, yo, k1, ssk, k3, [k2, k2tog, k1, yo, k5, yo, k1, ssk, k5, k2tog, k1, yo, k5, yo, k1, ssk, k3], k2, k2tog, k1, yo, k5, yo, k1, ssk, k6, yo, k2.

Row 29: K2, yo, k6, k2tog, k1, yo, k2, yo, sl1, k2tog, psso, yo, k2, yo, k1, ssk, k2, [k1, k2tog, k1, yo, k2, yo, sl1, k2tog, psso, yo, k2, yo, k1, ssk, k3, k2tog, k1, yo, k2, yo, sl1, k2tog, psso, yo, k2, yo, k1, ssk, k2], k1, k2tog, k1, yo, k2, yo, sl1, k2tog, psso, yo, k2, yo, k1, ssk, k6, yo, k2.

Row 31: k2, yo, k2, k2tog, (k1, yo) 2 times, k1, ssk, k2, yo, ssk, B, k2tog, yo, k6, [k5, yo, ssk, B, k2tog, yo, k2, k2tog, (k1, yo) 2 times, k1, ssk, k2, yo, ssk, B, k2tog, yo, k6], k5, yo, ssk, B, k2tog, yo, k2, k2tog, (k1, yo) 2 times, k1, ssk, k2, yo, k2.

Row 33: k2, yo, k2, k2tog, k1, yo, k3, yo, k1, ssk, k2, yo, sl1, k2tog, psso, yo, k7, [k6, yo, sl1, k2tog, psso, yo, k2, k2tog, k1, yo, k3, yo, k1, ssk, k2, yo, sl1, k2tog, psso, yo, k7], k6, yo, sl1, k2tog, psso, yo, k2, k2tog, k1, yo, k3, yo, k1, ssk, k2, yo, k2.

Row 35: K2, yo, k2, k2tog, k1, yo, k5, yo, k1, ssk, k11, [k10, k2tog, k1, yo, k5, yo, k1, ssk, k11], k10, k2tog, k1, yo, k5, yo, k1, ssk, k2, yo, k2.

Row 37: K2, yo, k2, k2tog, k1, yo, k2, yo, sl1, k2tog, psso, yo, k2, yo, k1, ssk, k10, [k9, k2tog, k1, yo, k2, yo, sl1, k2tog, psso, yo, k2, yo, k1, ssk, k10], k9, k2tog, k1, yo, k2, yo, sl1, k2tog, psso, yo, k2, yo, k1, ssk, k2, yo, k2.

Row 39: K2, yo, k7, yo, ssk, B, k2tog, yo, k14, [k13, yo, ssk, B, k2tog, yo, k14], k13, yo, ssk, B, k2tog, yo, k7, yo, k2.

Row 41: K2, yo, k9, yo, sl1, k2tog, psso, yo, k15, [k14, yo, sl1, k2tog, psso, yo, k15], k14, yo, sl1, k2tog, psso, yo, k9, yo, k2.

Chart C

Pattern repeat is in [ ].

Row 1 (RS): K2, yo, k1, k2tog, yo, k1, yo, ssk, k11, k2tog, yo, k1, yo, ssk, k6, [k5, k2tog, yo, k1, yo, ssk, k11, k2tog, yo, k1,

yo, ssk, k6], k5, k2tog, yo, k1, yo, ssk, k11, k2tog, yo, k1, yo, ssk, k1, yo, k2.

Row 2 and all WS rows: K2, p to last 2 sts, k2.

Row 3: K2, yo, k1, k2tog, yo, k3, yo, ssk, k9, k2tog, yo, k3, yo, ssk, k5, [k4, k2tog, yo, k3, yo, ssk, k9, k2tog, yo, k3, yo, ssk, k5], k4, k2tog, yo, k3, yo, ssk, k9, k2tog, yo, k3, yo, ssk, k1, yo, k2.

Row 5: K2, yo, k1, k2tog, yo, k5, yo, ssk, k7, k2tog, yo, k5, yo, ssk, k4, [k3, k2tog, yo, k5, yo, ssk, k7, k2tog, yo, k5, yo, ssk, k4], k3, k2tog, yo, k5, yo, ssk, k7, k2tog, yo, k5, yo, ssk, k1, yo, k2.

Row 7: K2, yo, k1, k2tog, yo, k7, yo, ssk, k2tog, yo, k1, yo, ssk, k2tog, yo, k7, yo, ssk, k3, [k2, k2tog, yo, k7, yo, ssk, k2tog, yo, k1, yo, ssk, k2tog, yo, k7, yo, ssk, k3], k2, k2tog, yo, k7, yo, ssk, k2tog, yo, k1, yo, ssk, k2tog, yo, k7, yo, ssk, k1, yo, k2.

Row 9: K2, yo, k1, k2tog, yo, k4, B, k4, k2tog, yo, k3, yo, ssk, k4, B, k4, yo, ssk, k2, [k1, k2tog, yo, k4, B, k4, k2tog, yo, k3, yo, ssk, k4, B, k4, yo, ssk, k2], k1, k2tog, yo, k4, B, k4, k2tog, yo, k3, yo, ssk, k4, B, k4, yo, ssk, k1, yo, k2.

Row 11: K2, yo, ssk, k1, yo, ssk, k7, k2tog, yo, k5, yo, ssk, k7, k2tog, yo, k3, [k2, yo, ssk, k7, k2tog, yo, k5, yo, ssk, k7, k2tog, yo, k3], k2, yo, ssk, k7, k2tog, yo, k5, yo, ssk, k7, k2tog, yo, k1, k2tog, yo, k2.

Row 13: K2, yo, ssk, k2, yo, ssk, k1, k2tog, yo, k2, k2tog, yo, k7, yo, ssk, k1, k2tog, yo, k2, k2tog, yo, k4, [k3, yo, ssk, k1, k2tog, yo, k2, k2tog, yo, k7, yo, ssk, k1, k2tog, yo, k2, k2tog, yo, k4], k3, yo, ssk, k1, k2tog, yo, k2, k2tog, yo, k7, yo, ssk, k1, k2tog, yo, k2, k2tog, yo, k2.

Row 15: K2, yo, ssk, k3, yo, sl1, k2tog, psso, yo, k1, yo, sl1, k2tog, psso, yo, k4, B, k4, yo, sl1, k2tog, psso, yo, k1, yo, sl1, k2tog, psso, yo, k5, [k4, yo, sl1, k2tog, psso, yo, k1, yo, sl1, k2tog, psso, yo, k4, B, k4, yo, sl1, k2tog, psso, yo, k1, yo, sl1, k2tog, psso, yo, k5], k4, yo, sl1, k2tog, psso, yo, k1, yo, sl1, k2tog, psso, yo, k4, B, k4, yo, sl1, k2tog, psso, yo, k1, yo, sl1, k2tog, psso, yo, k3, k2tog, yo, k2.

Row 17: K2, yo, ssk, k9, yo, ssk, k7, k2tog, yo, k11, [k10, yo, ssk, k7, k2tog, yo, k11], k10, yo, ssk, k7, k2tog, yo, k9, k2tog, yo, k2.

Row 19: K2, yo, ssk, k10, yo, ssk, k1, k2tog, yo, k2, k2tog, yo, k12, [k11, yo, ssk, k1, k2tog, yo, k2, k2tog, yo, k12], k11, yo, ssk, k1, k2tog, yo, k2, k2tog, yo, k10, k2tog, yo, k2.

Row 21: K2, yo, ssk, k11, yo, sl1, k2tog, psso, yo, k1, yo, sl1, k2tog, psso, yo, k13, [k12, yo, sl1, k2tog, psso, yo, k1, yo, sl1, k2tog, psso, yo, k13], k12, yo, sl1, k2tog, psso, yo, k1, yo, sl1, k2tog, psso, yo, k11, k2tog, yo, k2.

Row 23 (RS): K2, yo, ssk, k to last 4 sts, k2tog, yo, k2.

Key

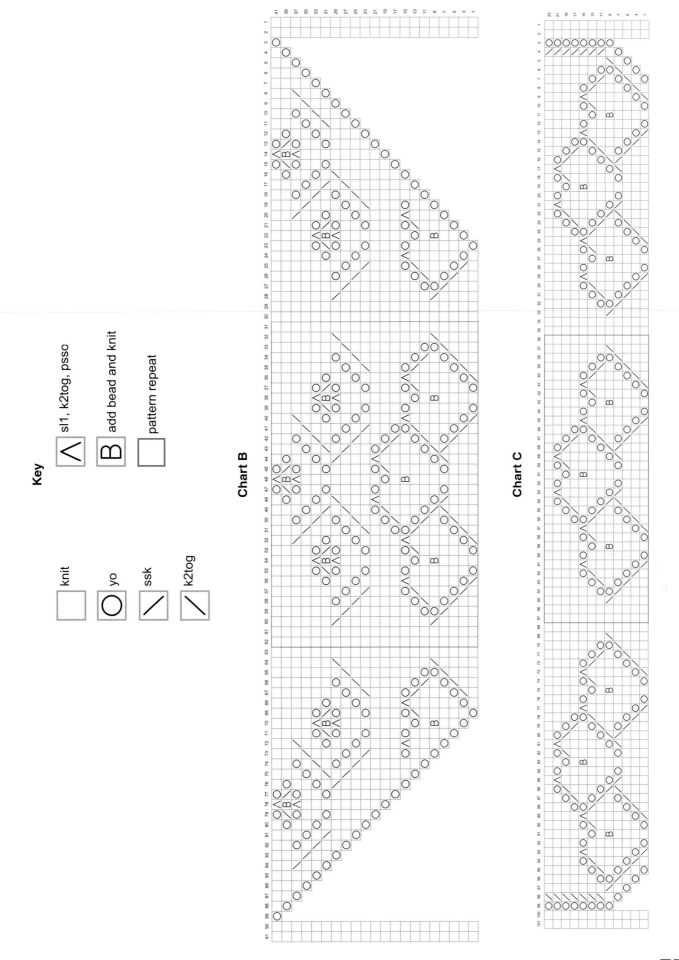

knit

yo

ssk

k2tog

$\wedge$ sl1, k2tog, psso

B add bead and knit

pattern repeat

Chart B

Chart C

Julia

The Julia hand warmers feature a beaded lace pattern with rib for a great fit and will look elegant and glamorous whether worn during shopping trips or out on the town for an evening.

FINISHED MEASUREMENTS

Hand circumference (measure at widest part):
Medium: To fit up to 8 in./20 cm hand circumference
Large: To fit up to 10 in./25 cm hand circumference
Length: $8^1/_2$ ($9^1/_2$) in./21.5 (24) cm (adjustable)

YARN

Lang Mille Colori Baby, fingering weight #1 yarn, 100% fine merino wool, 207 yd./190 m, 1.75 oz./50 g
- 1 ball #54

NEEDLES AND OTHER MATERIALS

- US 2 (2.75 mm) set of double-pointed needles
- 288 (342) ice blue size 6 seed beads (debbieabrahamsbeads.co.uk, #42)
- US 13 (0.75 mm) steel crochet hook (for adding beads)
- Stitch marker
- Tapestry needle

GAUGE

32 sts x 36 rows in Lace patt after blocking = 4 in./10 cm square
Be sure to check your gauge!

STITCH PATTERN

Lace Pattern

Row 1: P1, k1, k tbl, k1, yo, k1, k tbl, k1, p1.
Rows 2 and 4: P1, k7, p1.
Row 3: P1, k1, k2tog, yo, B, yo, ssk, k1, p1.
Row 5: P1, k2tog, yo, sl1, k2, psso, yo, ssk, p1.
Row 6: P1, k6, p1.

Key

knit	second stitch of sl1, k2, psso	add bead and knit
purl	sl1 k2 psso	k tbl
no stitch	k2tog	
yo	ssk	

Notes

- Stitch count changes on Row 1 of Lace patt chart (from 8 sts per pattern rep to 9 sts per pattern rep) and returns to normal on Row 5.
- Stitches are held for the thumb by working a number of stitches with a length of waste yarn, then slipping these stitches back onto the left needle and working them.
- See page 19 for a photo tutorial on Sewn Bind-Off.

Lace Pattern

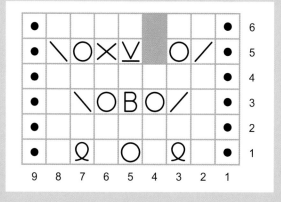

Both Hands

CO 48 (56) sts. Join to work in the rnd. Place a marker to mark beg of rnd.

Rnds 1–10: P1, k2, *p2, k2, rep from * to last st, p1.

Rnds 11–12: Work Row 1 of Lace patt 4 times (over 32 sts), p1, (k2, p2) 3 (5) times, k2, p1.

Rnds 13–17: Work Rows 2–6 of Lace patt as established.

Continue to work through all 6 rows of Lace patt 9 times in total. Work Row 1 of Lace patt once more.

Right Hand

Next rnd: Work Row 2 of Lace patt as set over 36 sts. Using a length of waste yarn, work the next 8 (10) sts in Rib patt as set. Slip these worked sts back to left needle and continue in patt as set using main yarn.

Left Hand

Next rnd: Work Row 2 of Lace patt as set over 36 sts. Work in Rib patt as set until last 8 (10) sts. Using a length of waste yarn, work 8 (10) sts in Rib patt as set. Slip these worked sts back to left needle and continue in patt as set using main yarn.

Continue in patt as set working all 6 rows of the Lace patt 3 (4) more times.

Next rnd: P1, k2, * p2, k2, rep from * to last st, p1.

Rep last rnd 4 more times.

BO using Sewn Bind-Off.

Thumbs

Undo the waste yarn and place 8 (10) sts from the bottom and 7 (9) sts from the top on 2 needles.

Rnd 1: Pick up and work in patt 1 (1) st, work in patt 8 (10) sts on the bottom needle, pick up and work in patt 2 (3) sts in the gap, work in patt 7, (9) sts from the top needle, pick up and work in patt 2 (1) sts—20 (24) sts.

Join to work in the rnd and continue in 2x2 rib for 8 (12) rnds or until the thumb is the desired length.

BO using Sewn Bind-Off.

Finishing

Weave in loose ends. Block the gloves if desired.

Atlantis is worked from the top down with a center insertion panel, which creates a shape that sits nicely on your shoulders.

Skill Level

Level 2

Notes

- Charts show RS rows only. See pattern for WS rows.
- See page 17 for a photo tutorial for Russian Bind-Off.

FINISHED MEASUREMENTS

Width: 56$^{1}/_{2}$ in./143.5 cm
Depth (center back): 23 in./58.5 cm

YARN

Malabrigo Sock, super fine weight #1 yarn, 100% super-wash merino wool, 440 yd./400 m, 3.5 oz./100 g
- 1 skein #474 Caribeno

NEEDLES AND OTHER MATERIALS

- US 6 (4 mm) needles (32 in./80 cm long circular needle recommended)
- 570 blue 4 mm miracle beads (framptonbeads.com)
- US 13 (0.75 mm) steel crochet hook (for adding beads)
- Tapestry needle

GAUGE

16.5 sts x 21 rows in Chart B patt after blocking = 4 in./10cm square
Be sure to check your gauge!

Cast On

CO 9 sts.
Knit one row.

Work Charts A and E

Row 1 (RS): K2, work Row 1 of Chart A, k1, work Row 1 of Chart E, k1, work Row 1 of Chart A, k2—6 sts inc'd.
Row 2 and all WS rows: K2, p to last 2 sts (purling the double yo's in Chart E as follows: p1, p1tbl), k2.
Row 3: K2, work Row 3 of Chart A, k1, work Row 3 of Chart E, k1, work Row 3 of Chart A, k2—6 sts inc'd.
Continue to work in patt through all 36 rows of Charts A and E once—99 sts.
NOTE: From Row 19 to end of chart, 4 sts inc'd every RS row.

Work Charts B and F

Row 1 (RS): K2, work Row 1 of Chart B working patt rep once, k1, work Row 1 of Chart F, k1, work Row 1 of Chart B working patt rep once, k2—4 sts inc'd.
Row 2 and all WS rows: K2, p to last 2 sts (purling the double yo's in Chart F as follows: p1, p1tbl), k2.
Row 3: K2, work Row 3 of Chart B working patt rep once, k1, work Row 3 of Chart F, k1, work Row 3 of Chart B working patt rep once, k2—4 sts inc'd.
Continue to work in patt through all 14 rows of Charts B and F a total of 3 times—183 sts. For each rep of Chart B, increase patt rep by one (for second repetition of Chart B, work patt rep 2 times, etc.).

Work Charts C and F

Row 1 (RS): K2, work Row 1 of Chart C working patt rep 4 times, k1, work Row 1 of Chart F, k1, work Row 1 of Chart C working patt rep 4 times, k2—4 sts inc'd.
Row 2 and all WS rows: K2, p to last 2 sts (purling the double yo's in Chart F as follows: p1, p1tbl), k2.
Row 3: K2, work Row 3 of Chart C working patt rep 4 times, k1, work Row 3 of Chart F, k1, work Row 3 of Chart C working patt rep 4 times, k2—4 sts inc'd.
Continue to work in patt through all 14 rows of Charts C and F a total of 3 times—267 sts. For each rep of Chart C, increase patt rep by one.

Work Charts D and G

Row 1 (RS): K2, work Row 1 of Chart D working patt rep 7 times, k1, work Row 1 of Chart G, k1, work Row 1 of Chart D working patt rep 7 times, k2—4 sts inc'd.
Row 2 and all WS rows: K2, p to last 2 sts, k2.
Row 3: K2, work Row 3 of Chart D working patt rep 7 times, k1, work Row 3 of Chart G, k1, work Row 3 of Chart D working patt rep 7 times, k2—4 sts inc'd.
Continue to work in patt through all 12 rows of Charts D and G once—291 sts.
BO using Russian Bind-Off.

Finishing

Weave in loose ends. Block shawl.

Chart A
Row 1 (RS): Yo, k1, yo.
Row 3: Yo, k3, yo.
Row 5: Yo, k5, yo.
Row 7: Yo, k7, yo.
Row 9: Yo, k3, k2tog, yo, k4, yo.
Row 11: Yo, k3, k2tog, yo, k1, yo, ssk, k3, yo.
Row 13: Yo, k1, yo, ssk, k2tog, yo, k3, yo, ssk, k2tog, yo, k1, yo.
Row 15: Yo, k3, yo, ssk, k5, k2tog, yo, k3, yo.
Row 17: Yo, k5, yo, ssk, k3, k2tog, yo, k5, yo.
Row 19: Yo, k7, yo, ssk, k1, k2tog, yo, k7, yo.
Row 21: Yo, k9, yo, sl1, k2tog, psso, yo, k9, yo.
Row 23: Yo, k3, k2tog, yo, k12, k2tog, yo, k4, yo.
Row 25: Yo, k3, k2tog, yo, k1, yo, ssk, k9, k2tog, yo, k1, yo, ssk, k3, yo.
Row 27: Yo, k1, (yo, ssk, k2tog, yo, k3) 3 times, yo, ssk, k2tog, yo, k1, yo.
Row 29: Yo, k3, yo, ssk, k5, k2tog, yo, k5, yo, ssk, k5, k2tog, yo, k3, yo.
Row 31: Yo, k5, yo, ssk, k3, k2tog, yo, k7, yo, ssk, k3, k2tog, yo, k5, yo.
Row 33: Yo, k7, yo, ssk, k1, k2tog, yo, k9, yo, ssk, k1, k2tog, yo, k7, yo.
Row 35: Yo, k9, yo, sl1, k2tog, psso, yo, k11, yo, sl1, k2tog, psso, yo, k9, yo.

Chart A

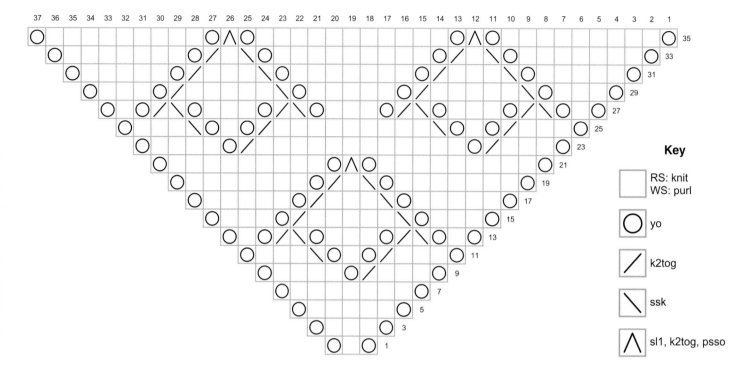

Key

	RS: knit WS: purl
O	yo
/	k2tog
\	ssk
∧	sl1, k2tog, psso

Chart B

Pattern repeat is in [ ].

Row 1 (RS): Yo, k3, k2tog, yo, k6, [k6, k2tog, yo, k6], k6, k2tog, yo, k4, yo.

Row 3: Yo, k3, k2tog, yo, k1, yo, ssk, k4, [k5, k2tog, yo, k1, yo, ssk, k4], k5, k2tog, yo, k1, yo, ssk, k3, yo.

Row 5: Yo, k1, yo, ssk, k2tog, yo, k3, yo, ssk, k2tog, yo, k1, [k2, yo, ssk, k2tog, yo, k3, yo, ssk, k2tog, yo, k1], k2, yo, ssk, k2tog, yo, k3, yo, ssk, k2tog, yo, k1, yo.

Row 7: Yo, k3, yo, ssk, k5, k2tog, yo, k2, [k3, yo, ssk, k5, k2tog, yo, k2], k3, yo, ssk, k5, k2tog, yo, k3, yo.

Row 9: Yo, k5, yo, ssk, k3, k2tog, yo, k3, [k4, yo, ssk, k3, k2tog, yo, k3], k4, yo, ssk, k3, k2tog, yo, k5, yo.

Row 11: Yo, k7, yo, ssk, k1, k2tog, yo, k4, [k5, yo, ssk, k1, k2tog, yo, k4], k5, yo, ssk, k1, k2tog, yo, k7, yo.

Row 13: Yo, k9, yo, sl1, k2tog, psso, yo, k5, [k6, yo, sl1, k2tog, psso, yo, k5], k6, yo, sl1, k2tog, psso, yo, k9, yo.

Chart C

Pattern repeat is in [ ].

Row 1 (RS): Yo, k2, k2tog, yo, k1, yo, ssk, k2, B, k1, [k2, B, k2, k2tog, yo, k1, yo, ssk, k2, B, k1], k2, B, k2, k2tog, yo, k1, yo, ssk, k2, yo.

Row 3: Yo, k2, k2tog, yo, k3, yo, ssk, k2, B, [k1, B, k2, k2tog, yo, k3, yo, ssk, k2, B], k1, B, k2, k2tog, yo, k3, yo, ssk, k2, yo.

Row 5: Yo, k2, k2tog, yo, k1, yo, sl1, k2tog, psso, yo, k1, yo, ssk, k2, [B, k2, k2tog, yo, k1, yo, sl1, k2tog, psso, yo, k1, yo,

ssk, k2], B, k2, k2tog, yo, k1, yo, sl1, k2tog, psso, yo, k1, yo, ssk, k2, yo.

Row 7: Yo, k1, B, k1, yo, sl1, k2tog, psso, yo, k3, yo, sl1, k2tog, psso, yo, k1, B, [k1, B, k1, yo, sl1, k2tog, psso, yo, k3, yo, sl1, k2tog, psso, yo, k1, B], k1, B, k1, yo, sl1, k2tog, psso, yo, k3, yo, sl1, k2tog, psso, yo, k1, B, k1, yo.

Row 9: Yo, k3, B, k1, yo, ssk, yo, sl1, k2tog, psso, yo, k2tog, yo, k1, B, k1, [k2, B, k1, yo, ssk, yo, sl1, k2tog, psso, yo, k2tog, yo, k1, B, k1], k2, B, k1, yo, ssk, yo, sl1, k2tog, psso, yo, k2tog, yo, k1, B, k3, yo.

Row 11: Yo, k5, B, k1, yo, ssk, k1, k2tog, yo, k1, B, k2, [k3, B, k1, yo, ssk, k1, k2tog, yo, k1, B, k2], k3, B, k1, yo, ssk, k1, k2tog, yo, k1, B, k5, yo.

Row 13: Yo, k7, B, k1, yo, sl1, k2tog, psso, yo, k1, B, k3, [k4, B, k1, yo, sl1, k2tog, psso, yo, k1, B, k3], k4, B, k1, yo, sl1, k2tog, psso, yo, k1, B, k7, yo.

Chart D

Pattern repeat is in [ ].

Row 1: Yo, k2tog, k2, yo, k1, yo, k2, ssk, B, k1, [k2, B, k2tog, k2, yo, k1, yo, k2, ssk, B, k1], k2, B, k2tog, k2, yo, k1, yo, k2, ssk, yo.

Row 3: Yo, k2tog, k2, yo, k3, yo, k2, ssk, B, [k1, B, k2tog, k2, yo, k3, yo, k2, ssk, B], k1, B, k2tog, k2, yo, k3, yo, k2, ssk, yo.

Row 5: Yo, k2tog, k2, yo, k5, yo, k2, ssk, [B, k2tog, k2, yo, k5, yo, k2, ssk], B, k2tog, k2, yo, k5, yo, k2, ssk, yo.

(continued)

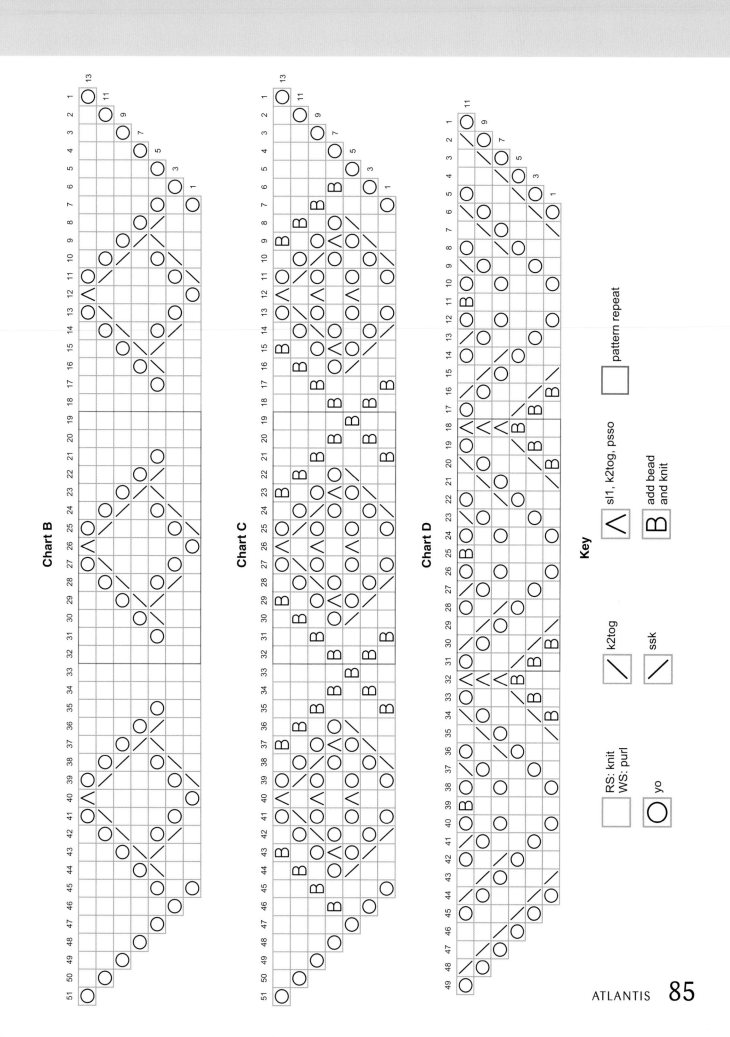

Chart B

Chart C

Chart D

Key

| | RS: knit
WS: purl | | sl1, k2tog, psso |
| | | | |

| | yo | | add bead
and knit |

| | k2tog | | pattern repeat |

| | ssk | | |

Row 7: Yo, k2tog, k2, yo, k2tog, (k1, yo) 2 times, k1, ssk, yo, k2, [sl1, k2tog, psso, k2, yo, k2tog, (k1, yo) 2 times, k1, ssk, yo, k2], sl1, k2tog, psso, k2, yo, k2tog, (k1, yo) 2 times, k1, ssk, yo, k2, ssk, yo.

Row 9: Yo, k2tog, k2, yo, k2tog, k1, yo, k3, yo, k1, ssk, yo, k1, [sl1, k2tog, psso, k1, yo, k2tog, k1, yo, k3, yo, k1, ssk, yo, k1], sl1, k2tog, psso, k1, yo, k2tog, k1, yo, k3, yo, k1, ssk, yo, k2, ssk, yo.

Row 11: Yo, k2tog, k2, yo, k2tog, k1, yo, k2tog, yo, B, yo, ssk, yo, k1, ssk, yo, [sl1, k2tog, psso, yo, k2tog, k1, yo, k2tog, yo, B, yo, ssk, yo, k1, ssk, yo], sl1, k2tog, psso, yo, k2tog, k1, yo, k2tog, yo, B, yo, ssk, yo, k1, ssk, yo, k2, ssk, yo.

Chart E

Row 1 (RS): Yo, k1, yo.
Row 3: Yo, k3, yo.
Row 5: Yo, k5, yo.
Row 7: Yo, k7, yo.
Row 9: Yo, k9, yo.
Row 11: Yo, k11, yo.

Row 13: Yo, k3, k2tog, (yo) 2 times, sl1, k2tog, psso, (yo) 2 times, ssk, k3, yo.
Row 15: Yo, k1, k2tog, (yo) 2 times, ssk, k1, k tbl, k2, k tbl, k2tog, (yo) 2 times, ssk, k1, yo.
Row 17: Yo, k4, k tbl, k2tog, (yo) 2 times, sl1, k2tog, psso, (yo) 2 times, ssk, k1, k tbl, k3, yo.
Row 19: Yo, ssk, k1, k2tog, (yo) 2 times, ssk, k1, k tbl, k2, k tbl, k2tog, (yo) 2 times, ssk, k1, k2tog, yo.
Row 21: Yo, ssk, k3, k tbl, k8, k tbl, k2, k2tog, yo.
Row 23: Yo, ssk, k15, k2tog, yo.
Row 25: Yo, ssk, k1, k2tog, (yo) 2 times, ssk, k5, k2tog, (yo) 2 times, ssk, k1, k2tog, yo.
Row 27: Yo, ssk, k3, k tbl, k2tog, (yo) 2 times, sl1, k2tog, psso, (yo) 2 times, ssk, k1, k tbl, k2, k2tog, yo.
Row 29: Yo, ssk, k1, k2tog, (yo) 2 times, ssk, k1, k tbl, k2, k tbl, k2tog, (yo) 2 times, ssk, k1, k2tog, yo.
Row 31: Yo, ssk, k3, k tbl, k2tog, (yo) 2 times, sl1, k2tog, psso, (yo) 2 times, ssk, k1, k tbl, k2, k2tog, yo.
Row 33: Yo, ssk, k1, k2tog, (yo) 2 times, ssk, k1, k tbl, k2, k tbl, k2tog, (yo) 2 times, ssk, k1, k2tog, yo.
Row 35: Yo, ssk, k3, k tbl, k8, k tbl, k2, k2tog, yo.

Chart E

Key

	RS: knit WS: purl
O	yo
/	k2tog
\	ssk
∧	sl1, k2tog, psso
Ω	RS: k tbl WS: p tbl

Chart F

Row 1: Yo, ssk, k15, k2tog, yo.

Row 3: Yo, ssk, k1, k2tog, (yo) 2 times, ssk, k5, k2tog, (yo) 2 times, ssk, k1, k2tog, yo.

Row 5: Yo, ssk, k3, k tbl, k2tog, (yo) 2 times, sl1, k2tog, psso, (yo) 2 times, ssk, k1, k tbl, k2, k2tog, yo.

Row 7: Yo, ssk, k1, k2tog, (yo) 2 times, ssk, k1, k tbl, k2, k tbl, k2tog, (yo) 2 times, ssk, k1, k2tog, yo.

Row 9: Yo, ssk, k3, k tbl, k2tog, (yo) 2 times, sl1, k2tog, psso, (yo) 2 times, ssk, k1, k tbl, k2, k2tog, yo.

Row 11: Yo, ssk, k1, k2tog, (yo) 2 times, ssk, k1, k tbl, k2, k tbl, k2tog, (yo) 2 times, ssk, k1, k2tog, yo.

Row 13: Yo, ssk, k3, k tbl, k8, k tbl, k2, k2tog, yo.

Chart G

Row 1: Yo, ssk, k3, k2tog, k2, yo, k1, yo, k2, ssk, k3, k2tog, yo.

Row 3: Yo, ssk, k2, k2tog, k2, yo, k3, yo, k2, ssk, k2, k2tog, yo.

Row 5: Yo, ssk, k1, k2tog, k2, yo, k5, yo, k2, ssk, k1, k2tog, yo.

Row 7: Yo, ssk, k2tog, k2, yo, k2tog, (k1, yo) 2 times, k1, ssk, yo, k2, ssk, k2tog, yo.

Row 9: Yo, sl1, k2tog, psso, k2, yo, k2tog, k1, yo, k3, yo, k1, ssk, yo, k2, sl1, k2tog, psso, yo.

Row 11: Yo, sl1, k2tog, psso, (k1, yo, k2tog) 2 times, yo, B, yo, (ssk, yo, k1) 2 times, sl1, k2tog, psso, yo.

Chart F

19	18	17	16	15	14	13	12	11	10	9	8	7	6	5	4	3	2	1	

Chart G

19	18	17	16	15	14	13	12	11	10	9	8	7	6	5	4	3	2	1	

Key

(blank)	RS: knit / WS: purl
O	yo
/	k2tog
\	ssk
∧	sl1, k2tog, psso
Ϙ	RS: k tbl / WS: p tbl
B	add bead and knit

Leah

A stunning lace pattern and twinkling beads give Leah a luxurious look. The crescent shape sits nicely on the shoulders and is an easy shape to wear. The shawl is finished off with a Crochet Chain Bind-Off (which is optional) to give it a traditional look.

FINISHED MEASUREMENTS
Inner crescent: 35$^{1}/_{2}$ in./90 cm
Outer crescent: 75 in./190.5 cm
Depth: 14$^{1}/_{2}$ in./37 cm

YARN
Tanis Fiber Arts Purple Label Cashmere Sock, fingering weight #1 yarn, 70% merino/20% cashmere/10% nylon, 400 yd./365 m, 4 oz./115 g
- 1 skein Jewel

NEEDLES AND OTHER MATERIALS
- US 6 (4 mm) circular needle, 32 in./80 cm long
- US G-6 (4 mm) crochet hook
- 444 lavender size 6 seed beads (debbieabrahamsbeads.co.uk, #337 Lavender)
- US 13 (0.75 mm) steel crochet hook (for adding beads)
- Tapestry needle

GAUGE
17 sts x 21 rows in Chart A patt after blocking = 4 in./10 cm square
Be sure to check your gauge!

Skill Level

Level 2

Notes

- This crescent-shaped shawl is worked from the top down.
- You want a stretchy cast-on; I recommend the Long-Tail Cast-On holding two needles together. For a photo tutorial on the Long-Tail Cast-On, see page 12.
- If you like, instead of the Crochet Chain Bind-Off, you can use the Russian Bind-Off; see page 17 for a photo tutorial.

Transition Section

Row 1 (RS): Sl wyif, k to end.
Row 2 (WS): Sl wyif, k1, p to last 2 sts, k2.
Row 3: Sl wyif, k1, *k2, (yo) 2 times, k5, (yo) 2 times, k3, (yo) 2 times, k5, (yo) 2 times, k1; rep from * to last 3 sts, k3— 389 sts.
Row 4: Sl wyif, k1, p1, *p1, (p3 tbl), p5, (p3 tbl), p3, (p3 tbl), p5, (p3 tbl), p2; rep from * to last 2 sts, k2.

Work Chart B

Row 1 (RS): Work Row 1 of Chart B, working patt rep 24 times.
Continue to work in patt through all 14 rows of Chart B once.
Do not bind off and do not break yarn.

Crochet Chain Bind-Off

Using the larger crochet hook, *insert hook pwise into 5 sts, pull them onto hook, yo, and pull through all 5 sts, ch10, insert hook into next 4 sts, pull onto hook, yo, and pull through all 4 sts, ch10, insert hook into 3 sts, pull onto hook, yo, and pull through 3 sts, ch10, insert hook into 4 sts, pull onto hook, yo, and pull through 4 sts, ch10; rep from * to last 5 sts on knitting needle, insert hook into last 5 sts, yo, pull through 5 sts, and pull off the needle. Fasten off.

Finishing

Weave in all loose ends. Block shawl.

Chart A
Pattern repeat is in [ ].
Row 1 (RS): Sl wyif, k1, [k5, yo, ssk, k1, k2tog, yo, k1, yo, ssk, k1, k2tog, yo, k4] 12 times, k3.
Rows 2, 4, 6, 8, 10, and 12: Sl wyif, k1, p to last 2 sts, k2.
Row 3: Sl wyif, k1, [k6, yo, sl1, k2tog, psso, yo, k3, yo, sl1, k2tog, psso, yo, k5] 12 times, k3.
Row 5: Sl wyif, k1, [k1, yo, ssk, k3, k2tog, yo, k2, B, k2, yo, ssk, k3, k2tog, yo] 12 times, k3.
Row 7: Sl wyif, k1, [k2, yo, ssk, k1, k2tog, yo, k2, B, k1, B, k2, yo, ssk, k1, k2tog, yo, k1] 12 times, k3.
Row 9: Sl wyif, k1, [k3, yo, sl1, k2tog, psso, yo, k2, B, k3, B, k2, yo, sl1, k2tog, psso, yo, k2] 12 times, k3.
Row 11: Sl wyif, k1, [k4, yo, ssk, k1, B, k5, B, k1, k2tog, yo, k3] 12 times, k3.
Row 13: Sl wyif, k1, [k1, yo, k4, ssk, k7, k2tog, k4, yo] 12 times, k3.

Cast On and Increase

CO 83 sts.
Row 1 (RS): K1, (k1, yo, k1) in each st to last st, k1—245 sts.
Row 2 (WS): Sl wyif, k1, p to last 2 sts, k2.

Work Chart A

Row 1: Work Row 1 of Chart A, working patt rep 12 times.
Continue to work in patt through all 16 rows of Chart A a total of 3 times.

Row 14: Sl wyif, k1, p1, [p1, yo, p4, p2tog, p5, ssp, p4, yo, p2] 12 times, k2.

Row 15: Sl wyif, k1, [k3, yo, k4, ssk, k3, k2tog, k4, yo, k2] 12 times, k3.

Row 16: Sl wyif, k1, p1, [p3, yo, p4, p2tog, p1, ssp, p4, yo, p4] 12 times, k2.

Chart B

Pattern repeat is in [ ].

Row 1 (RS): Sl wyif, k1, [k1, yo, B, ssk, k9, k2tog, B, yo] 24 times, k3.

Row 2 (WS): Sl wyif, k1, p to last 2 sts, k2.

Row 3: Sl wyif, k1, [k2, yo, k1, ssk, k2tog, (yo) 2 times, sl1, k2tog, psso, (yo) 2 times, ssk, k2tog, k1, yo, k1] 24 times, k3.

Row 4: Sl wyif, k1, p1, [p6, p tbl, p2, p tbl, p6] 24 times, k2.

Row 5: Sl wyif, k1, [k3, yo, B, ssk, k5, k2tog, B, yo, k2] 24 times, k3.

Rows 6, 8, 10, 12, and 14: Sl wyif, k1, p to last 2 sts, k2.

Row 7: Sl wyif, k1, [k1, (yo, k1, ssk) 2 times, k3, (k2tog, k1, yo) 2 times] 24 times, k3.

Row 9: Sl wyif, k1, [k2, (yo, B, ssk) 2 times, k1, (k2tog, B, yo) 2 times, k1] 24 times, k3.

Row 11: Sl wyif, k1, [k1, yo, (ssk, yo, k1) 2 times, sl1, k2tog, psso, (k1, yo, k2tog) 2 times, yo] 24 times, k3.

Row 13: Sl wyif, k1, [k2, yo, ssk, yo, k1, ssk, yo, sl1, k2tog, psso, yo, k2tog, k1, yo, k2tog, yo, k1] 24 times, k3.

Key

□	RS: knit / WS: purl
○	RS/WS: yo
╱	RS: k2tog / WS: p2tog
╲	RS: ssk / WS: ssp
∧	RS: Sl, k2tog, psso
B	RS: add bead and knit
Ω	WS: p tbl
V̇	RS/WS: slip purlwise with yarn in front
●	WS: knit
□	pattern repeat

Chart A

Chart B

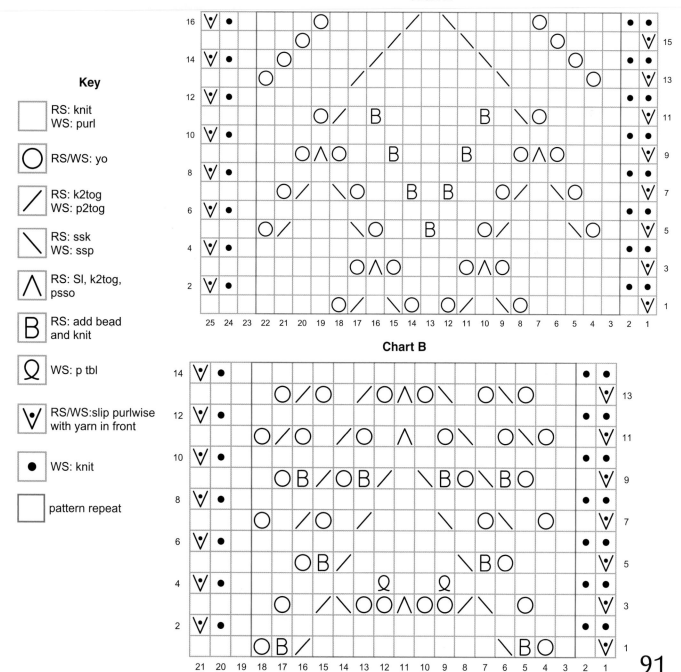

Ursula

The long color repeats of this self-striping yarn highlight the asymmetrical shape of the shawl, which is worked sideways. A beaded fan lace pattern edges two sides of it.

FINISHED MEASUREMENTS
Length: 56 in./142 cm
Depth (at the lace end): 26 in./66 cm

YARN
Schoppel Wolle Zauberball 100, super fine weight #1 yarn, 100% wool, 440 yd./400 m, 3.5 oz./100 g
- 1 skein #2170

NEEDLES AND OTHER MATERIALS
- US 6 (4 mm) straight or circular needles
- 249 lavender size 6 seed beads (debbieabrahamsbeads.co.uk, #337 Lavender)
- US 13 (0.75 mm) steel crochet hook (for adding beads)
- Tapestry needle

GAUGE
17 sts x 26 rows in Chart B patt after blocking = 4 in./10 cm square
Be sure to check your gauge!

SPECIAL STITCHES
Ssp: Slip 1 st knitwise, slip another st knitwise, slip both sts back to LH needle and ptog tbl—1 st dec'd.

Skill Level
Level 2

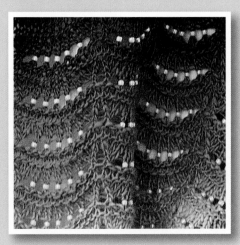

Notes

- See page 17 for a photo tutorial for Russian Bind-Off.

Edging

Row 1 (RS): Work Row 1 of Chart B, working patt rep 7 times.

Row 2 (WS): Work Row 2 of Chart B, working patt rep 7 times.

Continue to work in patt through all 56 rows of Chart B once—110 sts.

BO using Russian Bind-Off.

Finishing

Weave in loose ends. Block shawl.

Chart A

Row 1 (RS): Sl wyif, kfb, k to end.
Row 2 (WS): Sl wyif, k to end.
Row 3: Sl wyif, k to end.
Row 4: Sl wyif, k1, p2tog, p9, ssp, k to end.
Row 5: Sl wyif, kfb, k to last 13 sts, ssk, k7, k2tog, k2.
Row 6: Sl wyif, k1, p2tog, p5, ssp, k to end.
Row 7: Sl wyif, k to last 8 sts, (yo, B) 5 times, yo, k3.
Row 8: Sl wyif, k to end.

Chart B

Row 1 (RS): Sl wyif, kfb, k to end.
Row 2 (WS): Sl wyif, k to end.
Row 3: Sl wyif, k to end.
Row 4: Sl wyif, k1, [p2tog, p9, ssp], k4.
Row 5: Sl wyif, kfb, k2, [ssk, k7, k2tog], k2.
Row 6: Sl wyif, k1, [p2tog, p5, ssp], k5.
Row 7: Sl wyif, k4, [k1, (yo, B) 5 times, yo, k1], k2.
Row 8: Sl wyif, k to end.
Row 9: Sl wyif, kfb, k to end.
Rows 10–11: Sl wyif, k to end.
Row 12: Sl wyif, k1, [p2tog, p9, ssp], k6.
Row 13: Sl wyif, kfb, k4, [ssk, k7, k2tog], k2.
Row 14: Sl wyif, k1, [p2tog, p5, ssp], k7.
Row 15: Sl wyif, k6, [k1, (yo, B) 5 times, yo, k1], k2.
Row 16: Sl wyif, k to end.
Row 17: Sl wyif, kfb, k to end.
Rows 18–19: Sl wyif, k to end.
Row 20: Sl wyif, k1, [p2tog, p9, ssp], p2tog, p2, k4.
Row 21: Sl wyif, kfb, k3, k2tog, [ssk, k7, k2tog], k2.
Row 22: Sl wyif, k1, [p2tog, p5, ssp], p2tog, k5.
Row 23: Sl wyif, k2, (yo, B) 2 times, yo, k1, [k1, (yo, B) 5 times, yo, k1], k2.
Row 24: Sl wyif, k to end.

Body of Shawl

CO 18 sts.

Knit one row.

Row 1 (RS): Work Row 1 of Chart A, working patt rep until last 15 sts.

Row 2 (WS): Work Row 2 of Chart A.

Continue to work through all 8 rows of Chart A a total of 39 times—96 sts.

Row 25: Sl wyif, kfb, k to end.

Rows 26–27: Sl wyif, k to end.

Row 28: Sl wyif, k1, [p2tog, p9, ssp], p2tog, p2, k6.

Row 29: Sl wyif, kfb, k5, k2tog, [ssk, k7, k2tog], k2.

Row 30: Sl wyif, k1, [p2tog, p5, ssp], p2tog, k7.

Row 31: Sl wyif, k3, (B, yo) 3 times, k1, [k1, (yo, B) 5 times, yo, k1], k2.

Row 32: Sl wyif, k to end.

Row 33: Sl wyif, kfb, k to end.

Rows 34–35: Sl wyif, k to end.

Row 36: Sl wyif, k1, [p2tog, p9, ssp], p2tog, p2, k8.

Row 37: Sl wyif, kfb, k7, k2tog, [ssk, k7, k2tog], k2.

Row 38: Sl wyif, k1, [p2tog, p5, ssp], p2tog, k9.

Row 39: Sl wyif, k5, (B, yo) 3 times, k1, [k1, (yo, B) 5 times, yo, k1], k2.

Row 40: Sl wyif, k to end.

Row 41: Sl wyif, kfb, k to end.

Rows 42–43: Sl wyif, k to end.

Row 44: Sl wyif, k1, [p2tog, p9, ssp], p2tog, p2, k10.

Row 45: Sl wyif, kfb, k9, k2tog, [ssk, k7, k2tog], k2.

Row 46: Sl wyif, k1, [p2tog, p5, ssp], p2tog, k11.

Row 47: Sl wyif, k7, (B, yo) 3 times, k1, [k1, (yo, B) 5 times, yo, k1], k2.

Row 48: Sl wyif, k to end.

Row 49: Sl wyif, kfb, k to end.

Rows 50–51: Sl wyif, k to end.

Row 52: Sl wyif, k1, [p2tog, p9, ssp], p2tog, p9, ssp, k3.

Row 53: Sl wyif, kfb, k1, ssk, k7, k2tog, [ssk, k7, k2tog], k2.

Row 54: Sl wyif, k1, [p2tog, p5, ssp], p2tog, p5, ssp, k4.

Row 55: Sl wyif, k4, (yo, B) 5 times, yo, k1, [k1, (yo, B) 5 times, yo, k1], k2.

Row 56: Sl wyif, k to end.

Key

/	RS: k2tog / WS: p2tog
\	RS: ssk / WS: ssp
(grey)	no stitch
•	RS: purl / WS: knit
(blank)	RS: knit / WS: purl
V	RS: kfb
X	RS: stitch created by kfb
O	RS: yo
V̇	RS/WS: slip purlwise with yarn in front
(box)	pattern repeat
B	add bead and knit

Chart A

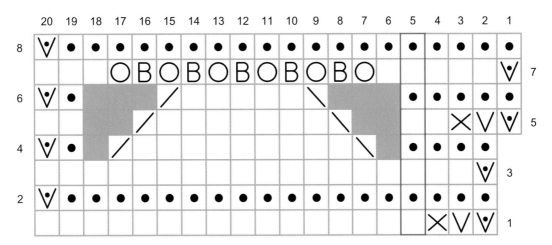

Chart B

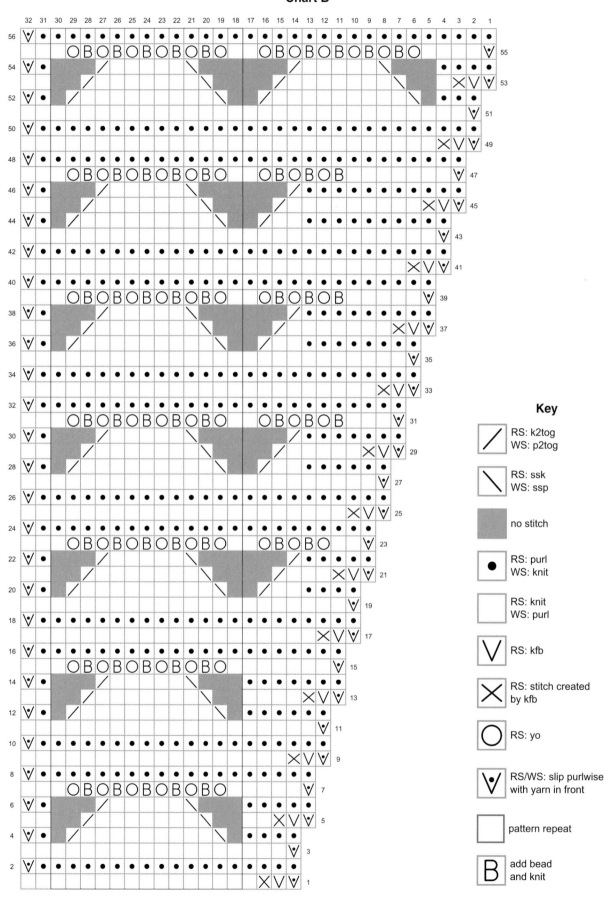

Key

╱	RS: k2tog WS: p2tog
╲	RS: ssk WS: ssp
▨	no stitch
●	RS: purl WS: knit
□	RS: knit WS: purl
V	RS: kfb
✕	RS: stitch created by kfb
O	RS: yo
V̇	RS/WS: slip purlwise with yarn in front
□	pattern repeat
B	add bead and knit

Dina

This triangular shawl features an interesting three-dimensional stitch pattern with lots of texture as well as beads around the edges.

Skill Level

Level 2

Notes

- This shawl is worked in rows from the bottom up. If you like, start with straight needles and switch to a circular needle if the number of stitches becomes too unwieldy.
- See page 17 for a photo tutorial for Russian Bind-Off.

FINISHED MEASUREMENTS

Width at the top: 59 in./150 cm
Depth: 33 in./84 cm

YARN

Cascade Yarns Heritage Silk, super fine weight #1 yarn, 85% superwash merino wool/15% mulberry silk, 437 yd./400 m, 3.5 oz./100 g

- 2 skeins #5627 Jade

NEEDLES AND OTHER MATERIALS

- US 6 (4 mm) circular needle, 32 in./80 cm long
- 252 size 6/0 teal beads (thebeadroom.co.uk, #17B)
- US 13 (0.75 mm) steel crochet hook (for adding beads)
- Tapestry needle

GAUGE

18.5 sts x 27.5 rows in Chart B patt after blocking = 4 in./10 cm square
Be sure to check your gauge!

SPECIAL STITCHES

Cable Cast-On (CCO): Insert RH needle between first 2 sts on LH needle, wrap yarn around needle and pull through to create a new st. Place new st on LH needle.

Cast On and Garter Stitch Edging

CO 9 sts.
Rows 1–4: K to end.

Work Chart A

Work through all 40 rows of Chart A once—57 sts.

Work Chart B

Row 1(RS): Work Row 1 of Chart B, working patt rep once.
Continue to work in patt through all 20 rows of Chart B a total of 9 times—273 sts. With each repeat of Chart B, add another patt rep (for the second rep of Chart B, work the patt rep 2 times, etc.).

Second Garter Stitch Edging

Rows 1–4: K to end.
BO using Russian Bind-Off.

Finishing

Weave in loose ends. Block shawl.

Chart A

Row 1 (RS): Sl wyif, k1, yo, k2tog, yo, p1, yo, ssk, yo, k2.
Row 2 (WS): Sl wyif, (k1, p3) 2 times, k2.
Row 3: Sl wyif, k1, yo, k2tog, yo, k1, p1, k1, yo, ssk, yo, k2.
Row 4: Sl wyif, (k1, p4) 2 times, k2.
Row 5: Sl wyif, k1, yo, k2tog, B, k1, yo, p1, yo, k1, B, ssk, yo, k2.
Row 6: Sl wyif, (k1, p5) 2 times, k2.
Row 7: Sl wyif, k1, yo, k2tog, B, k1, yo, k1, p1, k1, yo, k1, B, ssk, yo, k2.
Row 8: Sl wyif, (k1, p6) 2 times, k2.
Row 9: Sl wyif, k1, yo, k2tog, B, k1, yo, k2, p1, k2, yo, k1, B, ssk, yo, k2.
Row 10: Sl wyif, (k1, p7) 2 times, k2.
Row 11: Sl wyif, k1, yo, k2tog, B, k1, yo, k3, p1, k3, yo, k1, B, ssk, yo, k2.
Row 12: Sl wyif, (k1, p8) 2 times, k2.
Row 13: Sl wyif, k1, p1, k3, k2tog, B, k1, yo, p1, yo, k1, B, ssk, k3, p1, k2.
Row 14: Sl wyif, k2, p7, k1, p7, k3.
Row 15: Sl wyif, k1, p1, k2, k2tog, B, k1, yo, k1, p1, k1, yo, k1, B, ssk, k2, p1, k2.
Row 16: Sl wyif, k2, p7, k1, p7, k3.

Row 17: Sl wyif, k1, p1, yo, ssk, k1, (k2tog, yo) 2 times, p1, (yo, ssk) 2 times, k1, k2tog, yo, p1, k2.
Row 18: Sl wyif, k2, p7, k1, p7, k3.
Row 19: CCO 6 times, k2, p2, yo, sl1, k2tog, psso, yo, p1, yo, ssk, p1, k2tog, yo, p1, yo, sl1, k2tog, psso, yo, p2, k2.
Row 20: CCO 6 times, k4, p3, (k1, p2) 2 times, k1, p3, k10.
Row 21: Sl wyif, k1, yo, (k2tog, yo, p1, yo, ssk, p7) 2 times, k2tog, yo, p1, yo, ssk, yo, k2.
Row 22: Sl wyif, k1, p3, (k1, p2, k7, p2) 2 times, k1, p3, k2.
Row 23: Sl wyif, k1, yo, k2tog, yo, k1, p1, k1, yo, ssk, p6, yo, ssk, p1, k2tog, yo, p6, k2tog, yo, k1, p1, k1, yo, ssk, yo, k2.
Row 24: Sl wyif, k1, p4, k1, p3, k6, p2, k1, p2, k6, p3, k1, p4, k2.
Row 25: Sl wyif, k1, yo, k2tog, B, k1, yo, p1, yo, k1, B, ssk, p5, k2tog, yo, p1, yo, ssk, p5, k2tog, B, k1, yo, p1, yo, k1, B, ssk, yo, k2.
Row 26: Sl wyif, k1, p5, k1, p4, k5, p2, k1, p2, k5, p4, k1, p5, k2.
Row 27: Sl wyif, k1, yo, k2tog, B, k1, yo, k1, p1, k1, yo, k1, B, ssk, p4, yo, ssk, p1, k2tog, yo, p4, k2tog, B, k1, yo, k1, p1, k1, yo, k1, B, ssk, yo, k2.
Row 28: Sl wyif, k1, p6, k1, p5, k4, p2, k1, p2, k4, p5, k1, p6, k2.
Row 29: Sl wyif, k1, yo, k2tog, B, k1, yo, k2, p1, k2, yo, k1, B, ssk, p3, k2tog, yo, p1, yo, ssk, p3, k2tog, B, k1, yo, k2, p1, k2, yo, k1, B, ssk, yo, k2.
Row 30: Sl wyif, k1, p7, k1, p6, k3, p2, k1, p2, k3, p6, k1, p7, k2.
Row 31: Sl wyif, k1, yo, k2tog, B, k1, yo, k3, p1, k3, yo, k1, B, ssk, p2, yo, ssk, p1, k2tog, yo, p2, k2tog, B, k1, yo, k3, p1, k3, yo, k1, B, ssk, yo, k2.
Row 32: Sl wyif, k1, p8, k1, p7, k2, p2, k1, p2, k2, p7, k1, p8, k2.
Row 33: Sl wyif, k1, p1, k3, k2tog, B, k1, yo, p1, yo, k1, B, ssk, k3, p2, k2tog, yo, p1, yo, ssk, p2, k3, k2tog, B, k1, yo, p1, yo, k1, B, ssk, k3, p1, k2.
Row 34: Sl wyif, k2, p7, k1, p7, k2, p2, k1, p2, k2, p7, k1, p7, k3.
Row 35: Sl wyif, k1, p1, k2, k2tog, B, k1, yo, k1, p1, k1, yo, k1, B, ssk, k2, p2, yo, ssk, p1, k2tog, yo, p2, k2, k2tog, B, k1, yo, k1, p1, k1, yo, k1, B, ssk, k2, p1, k2.
Row 36: Sl wyif, k2, p7, k1, p7, k2, p2, k1, p2, k2, p7, k1, p7, k3.
Row 37: Sl wyif, k1, p1, yo, ssk, k1, (k2tog, yo) 2 times, p1, (yo, ssk) 2 times, k1, k2tog, yo, p2, k2tog, yo, p1, yo, ssk, p2, yo, ssk, k1, (k2tog, yo) 2 times, p1, (yo, ssk) 2 times, k1, k2tog, yo, p1, k2.
Row 38: Sl wyif, k2, p7, k1, p7, k2, p2, k1, p2, k2, p7, k1, p7, k3.

(continued)

Chart A

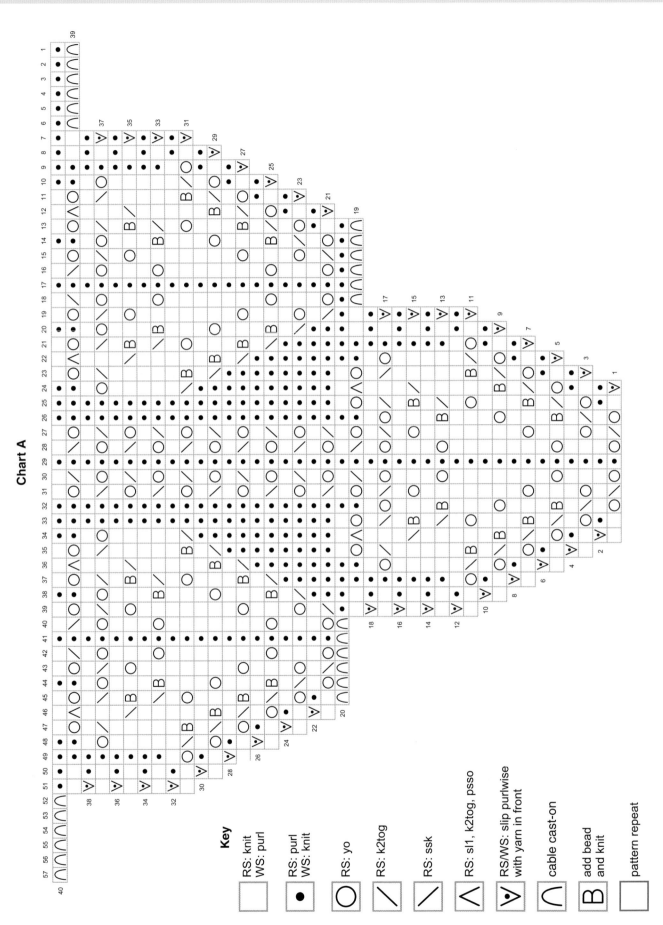

Key

RS: knit WS: purl	(blank box)
RS: purl WS: knit	●
RS: yo	○
RS: k2tog	/
RS: ssk	\
RS: sl1, k2tog, psso	/\
RS/WS: slip purlwise with yarn in front	>•
cable cast-on	∩
add bead and knit	B
pattern repeat	(blank box)

Chart B

Row 39: CCO 6 times, k2, p2, yo, sl1, k2tog, psso, yo, p1, yo, ssk, p1, k2tog, yo, p1, yo, sl1, k2tog, psso, yo, p3, yo, ssk, p1, k2tog, yo, p3, yo, sl1, k2tog, psso, yo, p1, yo, ssk, p1, k2tog, yo, p1, yo, sl1, k2tog, psso, yo, p2, k2.

Row 40: CCO 6 times, k4, p3, (k1, p2) 2 times, k1, p3, k3, p2, k1, p2, k3, p3, (k1, p2) 2 times, k1, p3, k10.

Chart B

Pattern repeat is in [ ].

Row 1 (RS): Sl wyif, k1, yo, k2tog, yo, p1, yo, ssk, p7, k2tog, yo, p1, [(yo, ssk, p7, k2tog, yo, p1) 2 times], yo, ssk, p7, k2tog, yo, p1, yo, ssk, yo, k2.

Row 2 (WS): Sl wyif, k1, p3, k1, p2, k7, p2, [(k1, p2, k7, p2) 2 times], k1, p2, k7, p2, k1, p3, k2.

Row 3: Sl wyif, k1, yo, k2tog, yo, k1, p1, k1, yo, ssk, p6, yo, ssk, p1, [k2tog, yo, p6, k2tog, yo, k1, p1, k1, yo, ssk, p6, yo, ssk, p1], k2tog, yo, p6, k2tog, yo, k1, p1, k1, yo, ssk, yo, k2.

Row 4: Sl wyif, k1, p4, k1, p3, k6, p2, [k1, p2, k6, p3, k1, p3, k6, p2], k1, p2, k6, p3, k1, p4, k2.

Row 5: Sl wyif, k1, yo, k2tog, B, k1, yo, p1, yo, k1, B, ssk, p5, k2tog, yo, p1, [yo, ssk, p5, k2tog, k2, yo, p1, yo, k2, ssk, p5, k2tog, yo, p1], yo, ssk, p5, k2tog, B, k1, yo, p1, yo, k1, B, ssk, yo, k2.

Row 6: Sl wyif, k1, p5, k1, p4, k5, p2, [k1, p2, k5, p4, k1, p4, k5, p2], k1, p2, k5, p4, k1, p5, k2.

Row 7: Sl wyif, k1, yo, k2tog, B, k1, yo, k1, p1, k1, yo, k1, B, ssk, p4, yo, ssk, p1, [k2tog, yo, p4, k2tog, k2, yo, k1, p1, k1, yo, k2, ssk, p4, yo, ssk, p1], k2tog, yo, p4, k2tog, B, k1, yo, k1, p1, k1, yo, k1, B, ssk, yo, k2.

Row 8: Sl wyif, k1, p6, k1, p5, k4, p2, [k1, p2, k4, p5, k1, p5, k4, p2], k1, p2, k4, p5, k1, p6, k2.

Row 9: Sl wyif, k1, yo, k2tog, B, k1, yo, k2, p1, k2, yo, k1, B, ssk, p3, k2tog, yo, p1, [yo, ssk, p3, k2tog, k2, yo, k2, p1, k2, yo, k2, ssk, p3, k2tog, yo, p1], yo, ssk, p3, k2tog, B, k1, yo, k2, p1, k2, yo, k1, B, ssk, yo, k2.

Row 10: Sl wyif, k1, p7, k1, p6, k3, p2, [k1, p2, k3, p6, k1, p6, k3, p2], k1, p2, k3, p6, k1, p7, k2.

Row 11: Sl wyif, k1, yo, k2tog, B, k1, yo, k3, p1, k3, yo, k1, B, ssk, p2, yo, ssk, p1, [k2tog, yo, p2, k2tog, k2, yo, k3, p1, k3, yo, k2, ssk, p2, yo, ssk, p1], k2tog, yo, p2, k2tog, B, k1, yo, k3, p1, k3, yo, k1, B, ssk, yo, k2.

Row 12: Sl wyif, k2, p7, k1, p7, k2, p2, [k1, p2, k2, p7, k1, p7, k2, p2], k1, p2, k2, p7, k1, p8, k2.

Row 13: Sl wyif, k1, p1, k3, k2tog, B, k1, yo, p1, yo, k1, B, ssk, k3, p2, k2tog, yo, p1, [yo, ssk, p2, k3, k2tog, k2, yo, p1, yo, k2, ssk, k3, p2, k2tog, yo, p1], yo, ssk, p2, k3, k2tog, B, k1, yo, p1, yo, k1, B, ssk, k3, p1, k2.

Row 14: Sl wyif, k2, p7, k1, p7, k2, p2, [k1, p2, k2, p7, k1, p7, k2, p2], k1, p2, k2, p7, k1, p7, k3.

(continued)

Row 15: Sl wyif, k1, p1, k2, k2tog, B, k1, yo, k1, p1, k1, yo, k1, B, ssk, k2, p2, yo, ssk, p1, [k2tog, yo, p2, k2, k2tog, k2, yo, k1, p1, k1, yo, k2, ssk, k2, p2, yo, ssk, p1], k2tog, yo, p2, k2, k2tog, B, k1, yo, k1, p1, k1, yo, k1, B, ssk, k2, p1, k2.

Row 16: Sl wyif, k2, p7, k1, p7, k2, p2, [k1, p2, k2, p7, k1, p7, k2, p2], k1, p2, k2, p7, k1, p7, k3.

Row 17: Sl wyif, k1, p1, yo, ssk, k1, (k2tog, yo) 2 times, p1, (yo, ssk) 2 times, k1, k2tog, yo, p2, k2tog, yo, p1, [yo, ssk, p2, yo, ssk, k1, (k2tog, yo) 2 times, p1, (yo, ssk) 2 times, k1, k2tog, yo, p2, k2tog, yo, p1], yo, ssk, p2, yo, ssk, k1, (k2tog, yo) 2 times, p1, (yo, ssk) 2 times, k1, k2tog, yo, p1, k2.

Row 18: Sl wyif, k2, p7, k1, p7, k2, p2, [k1, p2, k2, p7, k1, p7, k2, p2], k1, p2, k2, p7, k1, p7, k3.

Row 19: CCO 6 times, k2, p2, yo, sl1, k2tog, psso, yo, p1, yo, ssk, p1, k2tog, yo, p1, yo, sl1, k2tog, psso, yo, p3, yo, ssk, p1, [k2tog, yo, p3, yo, sl1, k2tog, psso, yo, p1, yo, ssk, p1, k2tog, yo, p1, yo, sl1, k2tog, psso, yo, p3, yo, ssk, p1], k2tog, yo, p3, yo, sl1, k2tog, psso, yo, p1, yo, ssk, p1, k2tog, yo, p1, yo, sl1, k2tog, psso, yo, p2, k2.

Row 20: CCO 6 times, k4, p3, (k1, p2) 2 times, k1, p3, k3, p2, [k1, p2, k3, p3, (k1, p2) 2 times, k1, p3, k3, p2], k1, p2, k3, p3, (k1, p2) 2 times, k1, p3, k10.

Janey

T his cardigan is knit in stockinette, with a beaded lace pattern on both sides of the front opening and a wide lace panel (no beads) running up the center of the back. The sleeves are three-quarter length and there is shaping at the waist.

Skill Level

Level 2

Notes

- Charts show RS rows only; see pattern for WS rows.
- The shoulders of the cardigan are shaped using short rows; for a photo tutorial, see page 22.
- For a photo tutorial on Three-Needle Bind-Off, see page 18.

FINISHED MEASUREMENTS

Extra-Small (Small, Medium, Large, Extra Large)
Bust: 36 (40, 44, 48, 52) in./91.5 (101.5, 112, 122, 132) cm
Length: 23^1/$_2$ (24^1/$_2$, 25, 25^1/$_2$, 26) in./59.5 (62.5, 63.5, 65, 66) cm
Sleeve length to underarm: 14 (14^1/$_2$, 14^3/$_4$, 15, 15^1/$_4$) in./35.5 (37, 37.5, 38, 39) cm

YARN

Berroco Comfort Sock, super fine weight #1 yarn, 50% superfine nylon/50% superfine acrylic, 447 yd./412 m, 3.5 oz./100 g
- 3 (4, 4, 5, 6) skeins color #1813 Southland

NEEDLES AND OTHER MATERIALS

- US 3 (3.25 mm) straight needles
- US 3 (3.25 mm) circular needle, 32 in./80 cm or 40 in./100 cm long
- US 13 (0.75 mm) steel crochet hook (for adding beads)
- 400 to 450 size 6 baby blue seed beads (debbieabrahamsbeads.co.uk, #387)
- 5 stitch holders
- 8 (^{3}/$_4$ in./2 cm) buttons
- Stitch markers (optional)
- Tapestry needle

GAUGE

26 sts x 31 rows in St st after blocking = 4 in./10 cm square
Be sure to check your gauge!

SPECIAL STITCHES

One-Row Buttonhole: Work to the place where you need to start the buttonhole.

1. Take the yarn to the front between the needles, slip one stitch purlwise to the right needle, take the yarn to the back between the needles.
2. *Slip the next stitch purlwise and pass the first slipped stitch over. Repeat from * until you have bound off the required number of stitches (or more if you prefer a larger buttonhole). Slip the stitch remaining on the

right needle to the left needle and turn the work. The working yarn is now at the beginning of the left needle.

3. With yarn at the back, Cable Cast-On the number of stitches you bound off plus one stitch (if you bound off 3, then cast on 4). Before placing the last stitch on the left needle, bring the yarn to the front between the needles, place the stitch on the left needle, and turn the work.

4. Slip the first stitch on the left needle knitwise, pass the last cast-on stitch over it, and tighten the stitch. The buttonhole is now complete and the total stitch count has not been altered.

Cable Cast-On: Insert RH needle between first 2 sts on LH needle, wrap yarn around needle and pull through to create a new st. Place new st on LH needle.

Back

Using straight needles, CO 117 (131, 143, 157, 169) sts.
Rows 1–6: K to end.

Shape Waist

Row 1 (RS): K43 (50, 56, 63, 69), k2tog, pm, work Row 1 of Chart A, pm, ssk, k43 (50, 56, 63, 69)—2 sts dec'd.
Row 2 (WS): P to end.
Row 3: K to m, sm, work Row 3 of Chart A, sm, k to end.
Row 4: P to end.
Continue in patt, decreasing before first m and after second m, every 8th row 4 more times—107 (121, 133, 147, 159) sts.
Continue in patt for 10 rows.
Next row (RS): K to m, m1, sm, work chart, sm, m1, k to end—2 sts inc'd.
Work 9 rows in patt.
Rep last 10 rows 4 more times—117 (131, 143, 157, 169) sts.
Continue in patt until back measures 16 (17^3/$_4$, 17^1/$_2$, 17, 17) in./40.5 (45, 44.5, 43, 43) cm, ending with a WS row.

Shape Armhole

BO 6 (7, 8, 9, 10) sts at beg of next 2 rows—105 (117, 127, 139, 149) sts.
Next row (RS): K2, ssk, work in patt to last 4 sts, k2tog, k2—2 sts dec'd.
Next row (WS): P2, p2tog, p to last 4 sts, p2tog tbl, p2—2 sts dec'd.
Rep last 2 rows 1 (2, 4, 5, 5) more times—97 (105, 107, 115, 125) sts.

Continue decreasing on RS rows only 0 (2, 1, 2, 3) more times—97 (101, 105, 111, 119) sts.
Continue in patt until back measures 22 (23, 23^1/$_2$, 24, 24^1/$_2$) in./56 (58.5, 59.5, 61, 62.5) cm, ending with a WS row.

Shape Right Neck

Next row (RS): Work in patt for 25 (27, 28, 31, 34) sts, turn.
Next row (WS): P1, p2tog, p to end—1 st dec.
Next row: K to last 3 sts, k2tog, k1—1 st dec, 23 (25, 26, 29, 32) sts.

Shape Right Shoulder

Next row (WS): P16 (17, 18, 20, 21), w&t.
Next row (RS): K to end.
Next row: P8 (8, 9, 10, 11), w&t.
Next row: K to end.
Next row: P to end, including wraps as they appear.
Place sts on holder.

Shape Left Neck

Place 47 (47, 49, 49, 51) sts on holder for back neck. Reattach yarn at neck edge and k to end—25 (27, 28, 31, 34) sts.
Next row (WS): P to last 3 sts, p2tog tbl, p1—1 st dec'd.
Next row (RS): K1, ssk, k to end—1 st dec'd, 23 (25, 26, 29, 32) sts.
Next row: P to end.

Shape Left Shoulder

Next row (RS): K16 (17, 18, 20, 21), w&t.
Next row (WS): P to end.
Next row: K8 (8, 9, 10, 11), w&t.
Next row: P to end.
Next row: K to end, including wraps as they appear.
Place sts on holder.

Left Front

Using straight needles, CO 59 (66, 72, 79, 85) sts.
Rows 1–6: K to end.

Shape Waist

Row 1: K30 (37, 43, 50, 56), k2tog, pm, work Row 1 of Chart B—1 st dec'd.
Row 2: P to end.
Row 3: K to m, sm, work Row 3 of Chart A.
Row 4: P to end.
Continue in patt, decreasing as set before marker, every 8th row 4 more times—54 (61, 67, 74, 80) sts.

(continued)

Continue in patt for 10 rows.

Next row: K to m, m1, sm, work Chart B—1 st inc'd.

Work 9 rows in patt.

Rep last 10 rows 4 more times—59 (66, 72, 79, 85) sts.

Continue in patt until front matches back to armhole shaping, ending with a WS row.

Shape Armhole

BO 6 (7, 8, 9, 10) sts at beg of next row, work in patt to end—53 (59, 64, 70, 75) sts.

Next row (WS): P to end.

Next row (RS): K2, ssk, work in patt to end—1 st dec'd.

Next row (WS): P to last 4 sts, p2tog tbl, p2—1 st dec'd.

Rep last 2 rows 1 (2, 4, 5, 5) more times—49 (53, 54, 58, 63) sts.

Continue decreasing on RS rows only 0 (2, 1, 2, 3) more times—49 (51, 53, 56, 60) sts.

Continue in patt until Left Front measures 18^1/$_2$ (19, 19^1/$_4$, 19^1/$_2$, 19^1/$_2$) in./47 (48.5, 49, 49.5, 49.5) cm, ending with a WS row.

Shape Left Neck

Next row (RS): K to 2 sts before marker, k2tog, sm, work in patt to end—1 st dec'd.

Next row (WS): P to marker, sm, p2tog, p to end—1 st dec'd.

Rep last 2 rows 10 (10, 11, 11, 12) more times—27 (29, 29, 32, 34) sts.

Continue decreasing on RS rows only 4 (4, 3, 3, 2) more times—23 (25, 26, 29, 32) sts.

Continue in patt until Left Front matches Back to shoulder shaping, ending with a RS row.

Shape Left Shoulder

Next row (WS): P16 (17, 18, 20, 21), w&t.
Next row (RS): K to end.
Next row: P8 (8, 9, 10, 11), w&t.
Next row: K to end.
Next row: P to end, including wraps as they appear.
Place sts on holder.

Right Front

Using straight needles, CO 59 (66, 72, 79, 85) sts.
Rows 1–6: K to end.

Shape Waist

Row 1 (RS): Work Row 1 of Chart B, pm, ssk, k30 (37, 43, 50, 56)—1st dec'd.
Row 2 (WS): P to end.
Row 3: Work Row 3 of Chart B, sm, k to end.
Row 4: P to end.
Continue in patt, decreasing as set after marker, every 8th row 4 more times—54 (61, 68, 74, 80) sts.
Continue in patt for 10 rows.
Next row: Work Chart, sm, m1, k to end—1 st inc'd.
Work 9 rows in patt.
Rep last 10 rows 4 more times—59 (66, 72, 79, 85) sts.
Continue in patt until Right Front matches Back to armhole shaping, ending with a RS row.

Shape Armhole

BO 6, (7, 8, 9, 10) sts at beg of next row—53 (59, 64, 70, 75) sts.
Next row (RS): Work in patt to marker, sm, k to last 4 sts, k2tog, k2—1 st dec'd.
Next row (WS): P2, p2tog, p to end—1 st dec'd.
Rep last 2 rows 1 (2, 4, 5, 5) more times—49 (53, 54, 58, 63) sts.
Continue decreasing on RS rows only 0 (2, 1, 2, 3) more times—49 (51, 53, 56, 60) sts.
Continue in patt until Right Front matches Left Front to neck shaping, ending with a WS row.

Shape Right Neck

Next row (RS): Work in patt to m, sm, ssk, k to end—1 st dec'd.
Next row (WS): P to 2 sts before m, sm, p2tog tbl, p to end—1 st dec'd.
Rep last 2 rows 10 (10, 11, 11, 12) more times—27 (29, 29, 32, 34) sts.
Continue decreasing on RS rows only 4 (4, 3, 3, 2) more times—23 (25, 26, 29, 32) sts.
Continue in patt until Right Front matches Back to shoulder shaping, ending with a WS row.

Shape Right Shoulder

Next row (RS): K16 (17, 18, 20, 21), w&t.
Next row (WS): P to end.
Next row: K8 (8, 9, 10, 11), w&t.
Next row: P to end.
Next row: K to end, including wraps as they appear.
Place sts on holder.

Sleeves (make 2)

Using straight needles, CO 62 (65, 72, 75, 82) sts.
Rows 1–6: K to end.
Row 7 (RS): K to end.
Row 8 (WS): P to end.
Rows 7 and 8 set pattern for stockinette stitch. Work 8 rows in St st.
Next row (RS): K2, m1, k to last 2 sts, m1, k2—2 sts inc'd.
Work 9 (7, 7, 5, 5) rows in St st.
Rep last 10 rows 9 (11, 12, 17, 17) more times—82, (89, 98, 111, 118) sts.
Continue in St st until sleeve measures 14 (14^1/$_2$, 14^3/$_4$, 15, 15^1/$_4$) in./35.5 (37, 37.5, 38, 39) cm, ending with a WS row.

Shape Sleeve Cap

BO 6 (7, 8, 9, 10) sts on next 2 rows—70 (75, 82, 93, 98) sts.
Row 1 (RS): K2, ssk, k to last 4 sts, k2tog, k2—2 sts dec'd.
Row 2 (WS): P to end.
Rep last 2 rows 6 (5, 5, 5, 6) more times—56 (63, 70, 81, 84) sts.
Next row (RS): K2, ssk, k to last 4 sts, k2tog, k2—2 sts dec'd.
Next row (WS): P2, p2tog, p to last 4 sts, p2tog tbl, p2—2 sts dec'd.
Rep last 2 rows 7 (7, 8, 10, 10) more times—24 (31, 34, 37, 40) sts.
BO 3 (5, 5, 5, 5) sts at beg of next 2 rows.
BO 4 (5, 5, 5, 5) sts at beg of next 2 rows.
BO rem 10 (11, 14, 17, 20) sts.

Finishing

Block pieces to measurements. Join shoulders using Three-Needle Bind-Off with WS of pieces facing. Set in sleeves. Seam underarm and side seams.

Button Band

Using longer circular needle, starting at bottom right front with RS facing, pick up and k152 (158, 162, 166, 170) sts to right shoulder, pick up and k4 to back neck, transfer 47 (47, 49, 49, 51) sts held on st holder to left needle and knit, pick up and k4 sts to left shoulder, pick up and k152 (158, 162, 166, 170) sts along left front—359 (371, 381, 389, 399) sts.

Row 1(WS): Sl wyif, k to end.
Row 2 (RS): Sl wyif, k to end.
Rep Row 1.
Next row (RS): K5 (6, 7, 4, 5), work 4-st One-Row Button-hole, [k9 (9, 9, 10, 10), work 4-st One-Row Buttonhole] 7 times, k to end.
Next row: K to end.
BO all sts.
Weave in loose ends. Sew on buttons.

Chart A

Row 1 (RS): K2, yo, ssk, k3, k2tog, yo, k3, yo, sl1, k2tog, psso, yo, k3, yo, ssk, k3, k2tog, yo, k2.
Row 2 and all WS rows: P to end.
Row 3: K3, yo, ssk, k1, k2tog, yo, k4, yo, sl1, k2tog, psso, yo, k4, yo, ssk, k1, k2tog, yo, k3.
Row 5: K4, yo, sl1, k2tog, psso, (yo, k5, yo, sl1, k2tog, psso) 2 times, yo, k4.
Row 7: K4, yo, sl1, k2tog, psso, yo, k3, k2tog, yo, k3, yo, ssk, k3, yo, sl1, k2tog, psso, yo, k4.

Row 9: K4, yo, sl1, k2tog, psso, yo, k2, k2tog, yo, k5, yo, ssk, k2, yo, sl1, k2tog, psso, yo, k4.
Row 11: K8, k2tog, yo, k7, yo, ssk, k8.
Row 12: P to end.

Chart B

Row 1 (RS): K1, B, yo, ssk, k3, k2tog, yo, B, k2, yo, sl1, k2tog, psso, yo, k2, B, yo, ssk, k3, k2tog, yo, B, k1.
Row 2 and all WS rows: P to end.
Row 3: K2, B, yo, ssk, k1, k2tog, yo, B, k3, yo, sl1, k2tog, psso, yo, k3, B, yo, ssk, k1, k2tog, yo, B, k2.
Row 5: K3, B, yo, sl1, k2tog, psso, yo, B, k4, yo, sl1, k2tog, psso, yo, k4, B, yo, sl1, k2tog, psso, yo, B, k3.
Row 7: K3, B, yo, sl1, k2tog, psso, yo, B, k2, k2tog, yo, B, k1, B, yo, ssk, k2, B, yo, sl1, k2tog, psso, yo, B, k3.
Row 9: K3, B, yo, sl1, k2tog, psso, yo, B, k1, k2tog, yo, B, k3, B, yo, ssk, k1, B, yo, sl1, k2tog, psso, yo, B, k3.
Row 11: K8, k2tog, yo, B, k5, B, yo, ssk, k8.
Row 12: P to end.

Key

☐	knit	B	add bead and knit	╱	k2tog
◯	yo	∧	sl1, k2tog, psso	╲	ssk

Chart A

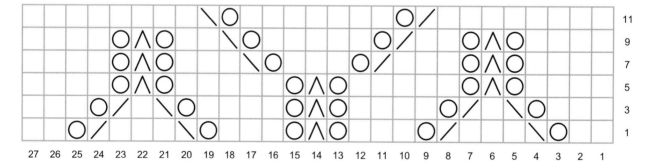

Chart B

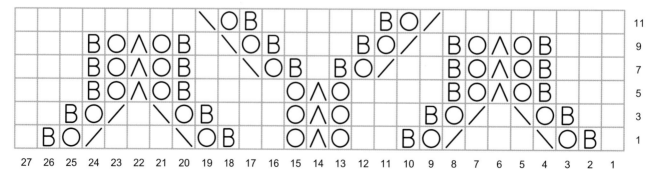

Helena

Helena is an elegant circular shawl with a swirling lace pattern and a beaded lace edging that is knitted on at the end instead of binding off the stitches. A fine lace weight yarn makes this shawl extremely light and airy.

Skill Level

Level 2

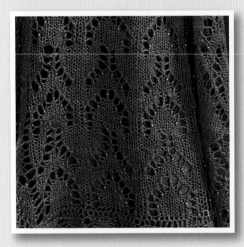

Notes

- This shawl is worked from the center out.
- Use a circular cast-on to begin the shawl. For photo tutorials, see pages 13–17. Move from dpns to progressively longer circular needles as the stitch count increases.
- For photo tutorials on provisional cast-ons and Kitchener Stitch, see pages 7 and 20.

FINISHED MEASUREMENTS

Width: $56^1/_2$ in./143.5 cm

YARN

Lorna's Laces Helen's Lace, lace weight #0 yarn, 50% silk/50% wool, 1,250 yd./1,143 m, 4 oz./114 g
- 1 skein Cranberry

NEEDLES AND OTHER MATERIALS

- US 4 (3.5 mm) set of double-pointed needles
- US 4 (3.5 mm) circular needles, 16 in./40 cm and 32 in./80 cm long
- 864 red size 8 seed beads (debbieabrahamsbeads.co.uk, #38 Red)
- US 15 (0.50 mm) steel crochet hook (for adding beads)
- Stitch marker
- Tapestry needle

GAUGE

18.5 sts x 27 rows in Chart B patt after blocking = 4 in./10 cm square
Be sure to check your gauge!

Cast On

Using a circular cast-on method, CO 8 sts. Divide sts evenly between 4 dpns, taking care not to twist them. Join to work in the rnd. Knit one rnd. Place a marker at beg of rnd.

Work Chart A

Rnd 1: Work Rnd 1 of Chart A—8 sts inc'd.
Rnd 2: Work Rnd 2 of Chart A.
Continue to work through all 46 rnds of Chart A once— 192 sts.

Work Chart B

Rnd 1: Work Rnd 1 of Chart B—8 sts inc'd.
Rnd 2: Work Rnd 2 of Chart B.
Continue to work through all 24 rnds of Chart B for a total of 3 times—480 sts.

Work Chart C

Rnd 1: Work Rnd 1 of Chart C a total of 8 times, working patt rep 5 times in each repeat of the rnd—8 sts inc'd.
Rnd 2: Work Rnd 2 of Chart C.
Rnd 3: Work Rnd 3 of Chart C a total of 8 times, working patt rep 5 times in each repeat of rnd—8 sts inc'd.
Continue to work in patt through all 24 rnds of Chart C for a total of 3 times; each time Chart C is repeated, work the patt rep one additional time for each repeat of the rnd (for the first repeat of Chart C, you will work patt rep 5 times in each repeat of the rnd, etc.) —768 sts.
Leave sts on circular needle. Do not bind off.

Edging

Using a provisional cast-on, CO 7 sts. Knit one row.
Row 1: Work Row 1 of Chart D, knitting the last st of the edging tog with 1 st of the main shawl (single join; make sure RS of main shawl is facing).
Row 2: Work Row 2 of Chart D.
Row 3: Work Row 3 of Chart D, knitting the last st of the edging tog with the next st of the main shawl (single join).
Row 4: Work Row 4 of Chart D.
Continue to work in patt through all 12 rows of Chart D a total of 128 times.
Do not bind off.

Finishing

Graft beginning and end of edging together using Kitchener stitch.
Weave in loose ends. Block shawl.

Chart A

Rnd 1: * K1, yo, rep from * to end.
Rnd 2 and all even-numbered rnds: K to end.
Rnd 3: *K2, yo, rep from * to end.
Rnd 5: *K3, yo, rep from * to end.
Rnd 7: *K4, yo, rep from * to end.
Rnd 9: * K5, yo, rep from * to end.
Rnd 11: *K6, yo, rep from * to end.
Rnd 13: *K7, yo, rep from * to end.

(continued)

Chart A

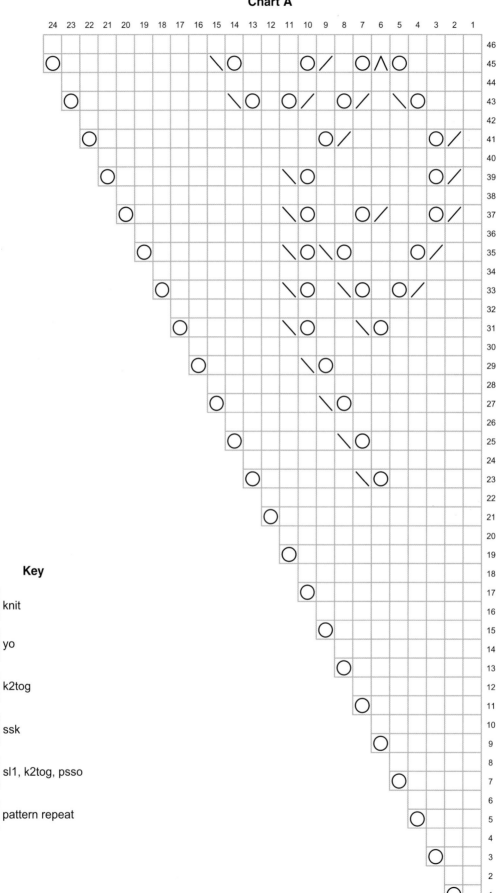

Key

knit

○ yo

／ k2tog

＼ ssk

∧ sl1, k2tog, psso

pattern repeat

Rnd 15: *K8, yo, rep from * to end.

Rnd 17: *K9, yo, rep from * to end.

Rnd 19: *K10, yo, rep from * to end.

Rnd 21: *K11, yo, rep from * to end.

Rnd 23: *K5, yo, ssk, k5, yo, rep from * to end.

Rnd 25: *K6, yo, ssk, k5, yo, rep from * to end.

Rnd 27: *K7, yo, ssk, k5, yo, rep from * to end.

Rnd 29: *K8, yo, ssk, k5, yo, rep from * to end.

Rnd 31: *K5, yo, ssk, k2, yo, ssk, k5, yo, rep from * to end.

Rnd 33: *K3, k2tog, yo, (k1, yo, ssk) 2 times, k6, yo, rep from * to end.

Rnd 35: *K2, k2tog, yo, k3, (yo, ssk) 2 times, k7, yo, rep from * to end.

Rnd 37: *K1, (k2tog, yo, k2) 2 times, yo, ssk, k8, yo, rep from * to end.

Rnd 39: *K1, k2tog, yo, k6, yo, ssk, k9, yo, rep from * to end.

Rnd 41: *K1, k2tog, yo, k4, k2tog, yo, k12, yo, rep from * to end.

Rnd 43: *K3, yo, ssk, (k1, k2tog, yo) 2 times, k1, yo, ssk, k8, yo, rep from * to end.

Rnd 45: *K4, yo, sl1, k2tog, psso, yo, k1, k2tog, yo, k3, yo, ssk, k8, yo, rep from * to end.

Chart B

Rnd 1: *K5, yo, ssk, k2, yo, ssk, k1, [k2tog, yo, k2, yo, sl1, k2tog, psso, yo, k5], yo, rep from * to end.

Rnd 2 and all even-numbered rnds: K to end.

Rnd 3: *K6, yo, ssk, k4, [k2, k2tog, yo, k3, yo, ssk, k3], k1, yo, rep from * to end.

Rnd 5: *K7, yo, ssk, k3, [k1, k2tog, yo, k4, k2tog, yo, k3], k2, yo, rep from * to end.

Rnd 7: *K8, yo, ssk, k2, [k2tog, yo, k5, k2tog, yo, k3], k2tog, yo, k1, yo, rep from * to end.

Rnd 9: *K5, yo, ssk, k2, yo, ssk, k1, [k2tog, yo, k1, k2tog, yo, k2, k2tog, yo, k3], k2tog, yo, k2, yo, rep from * to end.

Rnd 11: *K3, k2tog, yo, (k1, yo, ssk) 2 times, k1, [k2tog, yo, k1, yo, ssk, k1, k2tog, yo, k4], k2tog, yo, k3, yo, rep from * to end.

Rnd 13: *K2, k2tog, yo, k3, (yo, ssk) 2 times, k1, [k2tog, yo, k2, yo, sl1, k2tog, psso, yo, k5], k2tog, yo, k4, yo, rep from * to end.

Rnd 15: *K1, (k2tog, yo, k2) 2 times, yo, ssk, k1, [k2tog, yo, k3, yo, ssk, k5], k2tog, yo, k5, yo, rep from * to end.

Rnd 17: *K1, k2tog, yo, k6, yo, ssk, k1, [k2, yo, ssk, k8], k2, yo, ssk, k4, yo, rep from * to end.

(continued)

Chart B

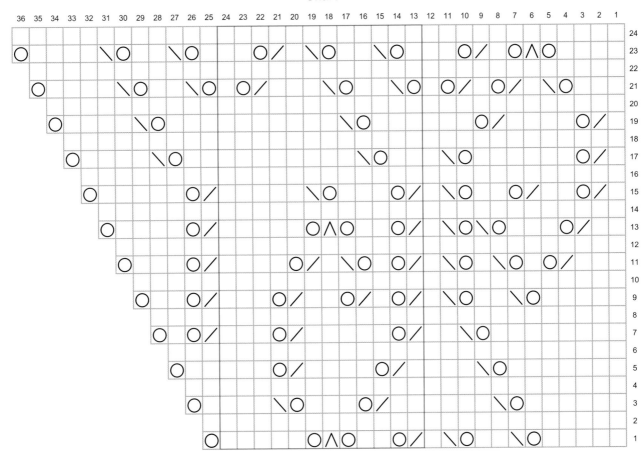

Rnd 19: *K1, k2tog, yo, k4, k2tog, yo, k3, [k3, yo, ssk, k7], k3, yo, ssk, k4, yo, rep from * to end.

Rnd 21: *K3, yo, ssk, (k1, k2tog, yo) 2 times, k1, [yo, ssk, k2, yo, ssk, k3, k2tog, yo, k1], yo, ssk, k2, yo, ssk, k4, yo, rep from * to end.

Rnd 23: *K4, yo, sl1, k2tog, psso, yo, k1, k2tog, yo, k2, [k1, yo, ssk, k2, yo, ssk, k1, k2tog, yo, k2], k1, yo, ssk, k2, yo, ssk, k4, yo, rep from * to end.

Chart C

Rnd 1: * [K4, yo, sl1, k2tog, psso, yo, k5], yo, rep from * to end.

Rnd 2 and all even-numbered rnds: K to end.

Rnd 3: * [K4, yo, sl1, k2tog, psso, yo, k5], k1, yo, rep from * to end.

Rnd 5: * [K4, yo, sl1, k2tog, psso, yo, k5], k2, yo, rep from * to end.

Rnd 7: * [K2, k2tog, yo, B, k1, B, yo, ssk, k3], k3, yo, rep from * to end.

Rnd 9: * [K1, k2tog, yo, k5, yo, ssk, k2], k4, yo, rep from * to end.

Rnd 11: * [K2tog, yo, B, k5, B, yo, ssk, k1], k5, yo, rep from * to end.

Rnd 13: * [K3, k2tog, yo, B, yo, ssk, k4], k3, k2tog, yo, B, yo, rep from * to end.

Rnd 15: * [K2, k2tog, yo, k3, yo, ssk, k3], k2, k2tog, yo, k3, yo, rep from * to end.

Rnd 17: * [K1, k2tog, yo, B, k3, B, yo, ssk, k2], k1, k2tog, yo, B, k4, yo, rep from * to end.

Rnd 19: * [K2tog, yo, k7, yo, ssk, k1], k2tog, yo, k1, yo, ssk, k4, yo, rep from * to end.

Rnd 21: * [K2tog, yo, B, k5, B, yo, ssk, k1], k2tog, yo, B, k1, yo, ssk, k4, yo, rep from * to end.

Rnd 23: * [K2tog, yo, k7, yo, ssk, k1], k2tog, yo, k3, yo, ssk, k4, yo, rep from * to end.

Key

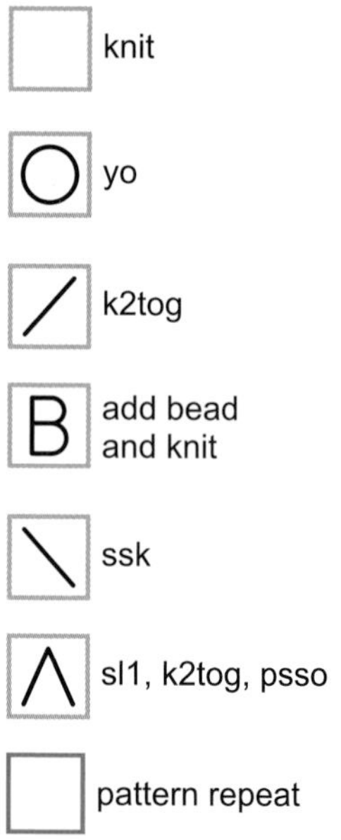

□	knit
O	yo
/	k2tog
B	add bead and knit
\	ssk
∧	sl1, k2tog, psso
□	pattern repeat

Chart C

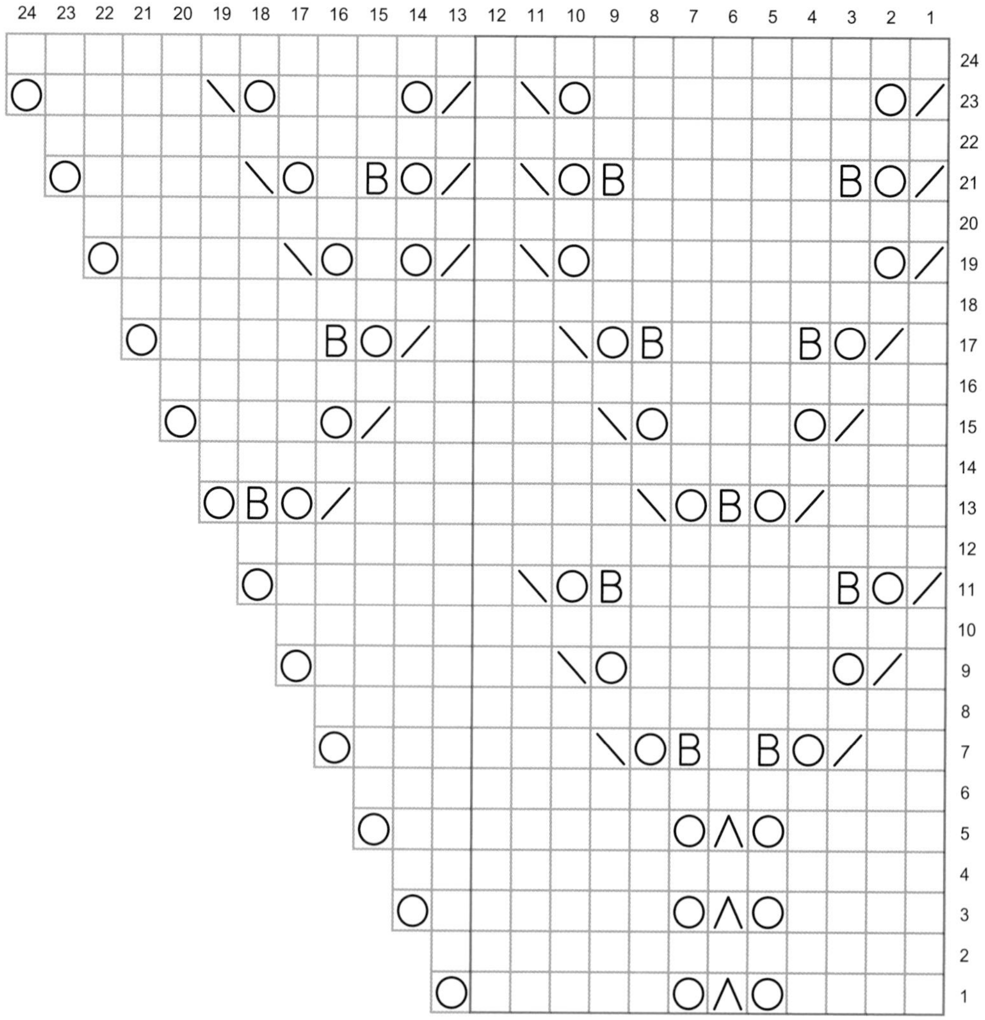

Chart D

Row 1 (RS): Sl wyif, k2tog, yo, k2, yo, B, SJ.
Row 2 (WS): Sl wyif, k2, k2tog, yo, k3.
Row 3: Sl wyif, k2tog, (yo, k2) 2 times, SJ.
Row 4: Sl wyif, k3, k2tog, yo, k3.
Row 5: Sl wyif, k2tog, yo, k2, yo, B, k2, SJ.
Row 6: Sl wyif, k4, k2tog, yo, k3.
Row 7: Sl wyif, k2tog, yo, k2, yo, k4, SJ.
Row 8: Sl wyif, k5, k2tog, yo, k3.
Row 9: Sl wyif, k2tog, yo, k2, yo, B, k4, SJ.
Row 10: Sl wyif, k6, k2tog, yo, k3.
Row 11: RBO 5 times, k5, SJ.
Row 12: Sl wyif, k6.

Key

☐	knit
⋒	single join
○	yo
∩	Russian bind-off
✕	st left from RBO
╱	k2tog
B	add bead and knit
⩔	slip purlwise with yarn in front
╲	ssk
☐	pattern repeat

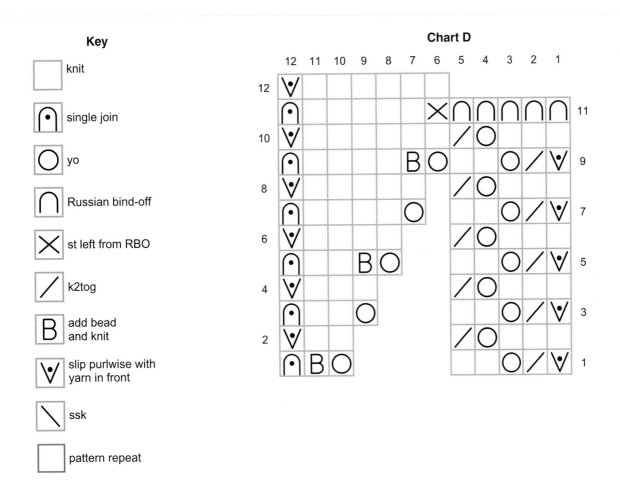

Chart D

HELENA 115

Maxine

Maxine is a stunning shawl with areas of true knitted lace (lace pattern worked on both right and wrong side rows). Beads are added for extra sparkle.

FINISHED MEASUREMENTS
Width: 29^1/$_2$ in./75 cm
Length: 60 in./152.5 cm

YARN
Classic Elite Yarn Silky Alpaca Lace, lace weight #0 yarn, 70% baby alpaca/30% silk, 460 yd./420 m, 1.75 oz./50 g
• 3 balls #2414 Lilac

NEEDLES AND OTHER MATERIALS
• US 4 (3.5 mm) circular or straight needles, any length
• US 4 (3.5 mm) double-pointed needles (2) or circular needle, 16 in./40 cm long
• 1,734 lavender size 8 seed beads (debbieabrahamsbeads.co.uk, #337 Lavender)
• US 15 (0.50 mm) steel crochet hook (for adding beads)
• Tapestry needle

GAUGE
17 sts x 27 rows in Chart A patt after blocking = 4 in./10 cm square
Be sure to check your gauge!

SPECIAL STITCHES
Single Join: Join one stitch of edging panel to one stitch of center panel (slipped sts on each long side or live stitches on short sides) by k2tog. Two edging rows are joined to one stitch of center panel.
Double Join: Work Single Join as above, on next RS row, work a second join in the same way and into the same center panel stitch. Four edging rows are joined to one stitch of center panel.

Skill Level
Level 3

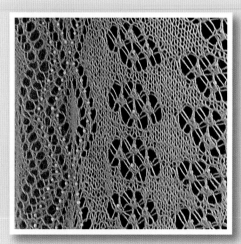

Notes

• The center panel of the shawl is worked first, and the edging knitted on afterward.
• Begin the shawl with a provisional cast-on; see pages 7–11 for photo tutorials.
• See page 20 for a photo tutorial for Kitchener Stitch.

Center Panel

Using a provisional cast-on and circular needle, CO 111 sts. Knit one row, k2tog in the middle of the row—110 sts.

Next row (RS): Work Row 1 of Chart A, working patt repeat 4 times.

Next row and all WS rows: Sl wyif, k to end.

Continue to work in patt through all 24 rows of Chart A a total of 17 times (408 rows).

NOTE: Place a removable stitch marker on the first st of Row 48.

Transfer sts to a st holder or length of waste yarn.

Edging

Using a provisional cast-on and the dpns or circular needle, CO 7 sts.

Knit 1 row, k2tog in the middle of the row—6 sts.

Work Chart B, working toward the cast-on edge of the center panel. Work first Single Join into the marked st of Row 48 on center panel.

Continue to work through and rep all 6 rows of Chart B to 3 sts before corner of center panel.

Corner 1: Work 3 Double Joins. Undo provisional cast-on, place 110 sts on a knitting needle, work 2 Double Joins into first 2 sts along cast-on edge. Work Chart B along short side to 2 sts before next corner of center panel.

Corner 2: Work 2 Double Joins. Start working along long side, work 3 Double Joins. Work Chart B along long side to 3 sts before next corner of center panel.

Corner 3: Work 3 Double Joins. Transfer 110 held sts to a needle, work 2 Double Joins. Work Chart B along short side to 2 sts before final corner.

Corner 4: Work 2 Double Joins. Start working along long side, work 3 Double Joins.

Continue working Chart B along final side until you reach the edging cast on. Undo provisional cast-on, place sts back on a needle and graft the two edges together using Kitchener stitch.

Finishing

Weave in loose ends. Block stole.

Chart A

Pattern repeat is in [ ].

Row 1 (RS): Sl wyif, k6, (k2tog, yo) 2 times, k1, B, k2tog, yo, B, k1, B, yo, ssk, k5, [k15], k5, k2tog, yo, B, k1, B, yo, ssk, B, k1, (yo, ssk) 2 times, k7.

Row 2 (WS): Sl wyif, k to end.

Row 3: Sl wyif, k5, (k2tog, yo) 2 times, k1, B, k2tog, yo, B, k3, B, yo, ssk, k4, [k5, k2tog, yo, k1, yo, ssk, k5], k4, k2tog, yo, B, k3, B, yo, ssk, B, k1, (yo, ssk) 2 times, k6.

Row 4: Sl wyif, k24, [k4, ssk, yo, k1, B, k1, yo, k2tog, k4], k25.

Row 5: Sl wyif, k4, (k2tog, yo) 2 times, k1, (B, k2tog, yo) 2 times, k1, yo, ssk, B, yo, ssk, k3, [k2, k2tog, yo, k1, yo, ssk, k1, k2tog, yo, k1, yo, ssk, k2], k3, k2tog, yo, B, k2tog, yo, k1, (yo, ssk, B) 2 times, k1, (yo, ssk) 2 times, k5.

Row 6: Sl wyif, k24, [k1, ssk, yo, k1, B, k1, yo, sl1, k2tog, psso, yo, k1, B, k1, yo, k2tog, k1], k25.

Row 7: Sl wyif, k3, (k2tog, yo) 2 times, k1, (B, k2tog, yo) 2 times, k3, yo, ssk, B, yo, ssk, k2, [k2, yo, ssk, k1, k2tog, yo, k1, yo, ssk, k1, k2tog, yo, k2], k2, k2tog, yo, B, k2tog, yo, k3, (yo, ssk, B) 2 times, k1, (yo, ssk) 2 times, k4.

Row 8: Sl wyif, k24, [k3, yo, sl1, k2tog, psso, yo, k1, B, k1, yo, sl1, k2tog, psso, yo, k3], k25.

Row 9: Sl wyif, k2, (k2tog, yo) 2 times, k1, (B, k2tog, yo) 2 times, k5, yo, ssk, B, yo, ssk, k1, [k5, yo, ssk, k1, k2tog, yo, k5], k1, k2tog, yo, B, k2tog, yo, k5, (yo, ssk, B) 2 times, k1, (yo, ssk) 2 times, k3.

Row 10: Sl wyif, k24, [k6, yo, sl1, k2tog, psso, yo, k6], k25.

(continued)

Key

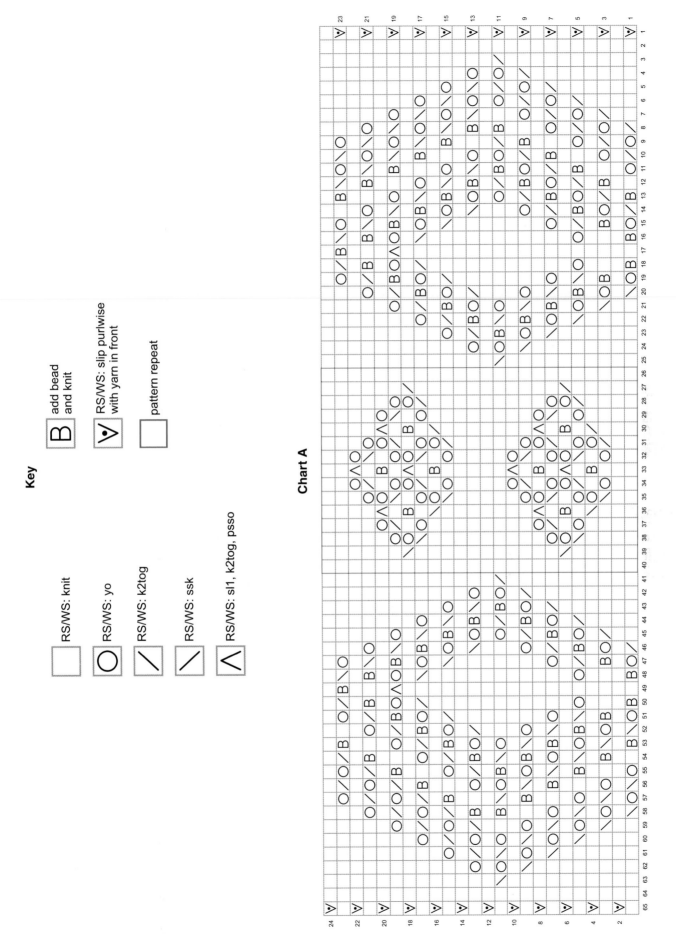	

RS/WS: knit

RS/WS: yo

RS/WS: k2tog

RS/WS: ssk

RS/WS: sl1, k2tog, psso

B add bead and knit

∨· RS/WS: slip purlwise with yarn in front

pattern repeat

Chart A

Row 11: Sl wyif, k1, (k2tog, yo) 2 times, k1, (B, k2tog, yo) 2 times, k7, yo, ssk, B, yo, ssk, [k15], k2tog, yo, B, k2tog, yo, k7, (yo, ssk, B) 2 times, k1, (yo, ssk) 2 times, k2.

Row 12: Sl wyif, k to end.

Row 13: Sl wyif, k2, (yo, ssk) 2 times, B, k1, yo, ssk, B, yo, ssk, k5, k2tog, yo, B, k2tog, yo, k1, [k15], k1, yo, ssk, B, yo, ssk, k5, k2tog, yo, B, k2tog, yo, k1, B, (k2tog, yo) 2 times, k3.

Row 14: Sl wyif, k to end.

Row 15: Sl wyif, k3, (yo, ssk) 2 times, B, k1, yo, ssk, B, yo, ssk, k3, k2tog, yo, B, k2tog, yo, k2, [k5, k2tog, yo, k1, yo, ssk, k5], k2, yo, ssk, B, yo, ssk, k3, k2tog, yo, B, k2tog, yo, k1, B, (k2tog, yo) 2 times, k4.

Row 16: Sl wyif, k24, [k4, ssk, yo, k1, B, k1, yo, k2tog, k4], k25.

Row 17: Sl wyif, k4, (yo, ssk) 2 times, B, k1, yo, ssk, B, yo, ssk, k1, k2tog, yo, B, k2tog, yo, k3, [k2, k2tog, yo, k1, yo, ssk, k1, k2tog, yo, k1, yo, ssk, k2], k3, yo, ssk, B, yo, ssk, k1, k2tog, yo, B, k2tog, yo, k1, B, (k2tog, yo) 2 times, k5.

Row 18: Sl wyif, k24, [k1, ssk, yo, k1, B, k1, yo, sl1, k2tog, psso, yo, k1, B, k1, yo, k2tog, k1], k25.

Row 19: Sl wyif, k5, (yo, ssk) 2 times, B, k1, yo, ssk, B, yo, sl1, k2tog, psso, yo, B, k2tog, yo, k4, [k2, yo, ssk, k1, k2tog, yo, k1, yo, ssk, k1, k2tog, yo, k2], k4, yo, ssk, B, yo, sl1, k2tog, psso, yo, B, k2tog, yo, k1, B, (k2tog, yo) 2 times, k6.

Row 20: Sl wyif, k24, [k3, yo, sl1, k2tog, psso, yo, k1, B, k1, yo, sl1, k2tog, psso, yo, k3], k25.

Row 21: Sl wyif, k6, yo, ssk, (yo, ssk, B, k1) 2 times, B, k2tog, yo, k5, [k5, yo, ssk, k1, k2tog, yo, k5], k5, yo, ssk, B, (k1, B, k2tog, yo) 2 times, k2tog, yo, k7.

Row 22: Sl wyif, k24, [k6, yo, sl1, k2tog, psso, yo, k6], k25.

Row 23: Sl wyif, k7, (yo, ssk) 2 times, B, k1, yo, ssk, B, k2tog, yo, k6, [k15], k6, yo, ssk, B, k2tog, yo, k1, B, (k2tog, yo) 2 times, k8.

Row 24: Sl wyif, k to end.

Chart B

Row 1 (RS): Sl wyif, k1, k2tog, yo, k1, SJ.

Row 2 (WS): Sl wyif, k2tog, yo, k1, (yo) 3 times, k2.

Row 3: Sl wyif, k2, k tbl, k1, k2tog, yo, k1, SJ.

Row 4: Sl wyif, k2tog, yo, k6.

Row 5: (RBO) 3 times, k1, k2tog, yo, k1, SJ.

Row 6: Sl wyif, k2tog, yo, k3.

Key

☐	RS/WS: knit
◯	RS/WS: yo
╱	RS/WS: k2tog
ⱽ	RS/WS: slip purlwise with yarn in front
∩•	single join
∩	Russian bind-off
✕	st left from RBO
Ϙ	k tbl

Chart B

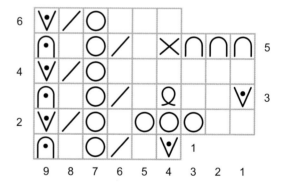

Catalina

This cape is worked from the top down with triple increases on Row 1, which creates an attractive crescent shape. It has an all-over lace pattern with beads on the lower half, followed by a pretty beaded edge and Crochet Chain Bind-Off.

Skill Level

Level 3

Notes

- You need a stretchy cast-on for this; use the Long-Tail Cast-On over two needles (page 12).
- In Rows 8 and 12 of Chart A, Rows 2, 10, and 18 of Chart B, and Rows 8, 12, and 16 of Chart C, the first time the pattern repeat is worked, the first stitch should be a purl. This is indicated on the charts by the purple box. In the written directions for these charts, the first repeat appears outside of the brackets indicating the pattern repeat.

FINISHED MEASUREMENTS

Small (Medium, Large)
Width (at top edge): 24$^1/_2$ (34$^1/_2$, 41) in./62 (88, 104) cm
Width (at lower edge): 49 (64, 82$^1/_2$) in./124.5 (162.5, 209.5) cm
Length: 22$^1/_2$ (22$^1/_2$, 22$^1/_2$) in./57 (57, 57) cm

YARN

Bijou Basin Ranch Bijou Spun Seraphim, lace weight #1 yarn, 95% angora/5% viscose, 435 yd./398 m, 1.75 oz./50 g
- 2 (3, 4) balls Eggplant

NEEDLES AND OTHER MATERIALS

- US 4 (3.5 mm) circular needle, 32 in./80 cm long
- US 4 (3 mm) crochet hook
- 962 (1,258, 1,628) rainbow-colored size 8 Japanese glass seed beads (thebeadroom.co.uk, #639 Rainbow)
- US 13 (0.75 mm) steel crochet hook (for adding beads)
- 1 small button
- Tapestry needle

GAUGE

17 sts x 25 rows in Chart C patt after blocking = 4 in./10 cm square
Be sure to check your gauge!

Cast On

CO 72 (94, 120) sts.

Row 1 (RS): K1 (1, 1), (k1, yo, k1) in each of next 70 (91, 118) sts, k1 (2, 1)—212, (276, 356) sts.

Row 2 (WS): K2, p to last 2 sts, k2.

Row 3: K to end.

Row 4: Rep Row 2.

Work Chart A

Row 1 (RS): Work Row 1 of Chart A, working patt rep 26 (34, 44) times.

Continue to work in patt through all 12 rows of Chart A for a total of 2 times.

Work through Rows 1–6 once more.

Next row (RS): K to end.

Next row (WS): K2, p to last 2 sts, k2.

Work Chart B

Row 1 (RS): Work Row 1 of Chart B, working patt rep 13 (17, 22) times.

Continue to work in patt through all 18 rows of Chart B once.

Next row (RS): K to end.

Next row (WS): K2, p to last 2 sts, k2.

Work Chart C

Row 1 (RS): Work Row 1 of Chart C, working patt rep 13 (17, 22) times.

Continue to work in patt through all 44 rows of Chart C for a total of 2 times.

Work Chart D

Row 1 (RS): Work Row 1 of Chart D, working patt rep 13 (17, 22) times—238 (310, 400) sts.

Continue to work in patt through all 10 rows of Chart D once.

Do not break yarn.

Crochet Chain Bind-Off

Using the larger crochet hook, insert hook into first 5 (5, 6) sts on LH needle, pull onto hook, yo, and pull through all 5 (5, 6) sts, ch10, *insert hook into next 4 sts, pull onto hook, yo, and pull through all 4 sts, ch10, rep from * to last 5 (5, 6) sts, insert hook into last 5 (5, 6) sts, pull onto hook, yo, and pull through all 5 (5, 6) sts.

Fasten off.

Finishing

Weave in loose ends. Block cape.

Chart A

Pattern repeat is in [ ].

Row 1 (RS): K2, [k2, k2tog, (yo) 2 times, ssk, k2], k2.
Row 2 (WS): K2, [p4, p1 tbl, p3], k2.
Row 3: K2, [(k2tog, (yo) 2 times, ssk) 2 times], k2.
Row 4: K2, [p2, p1 tbl, p3, p1 tbl, p1], k2.
Row 5: K2, [k2, k2tog, (yo) 2 times, ssk, k2], k2.
Row 6: K2, [p4, p1 tbl, p3], k2.
Row 7: K2, [yo, ssk, k4, k2tog, yo], k2.
Row 8: K2, p8, [p1 tbl, p7], k2.
Row 9: K2, [(k2tog, (yo) 2 times, ssk) 2 times], k2.
Row 10: K2, [p2, p1 tbl, p3, p1 tbl, p1], k2.
Row 11: K2, [yo, ssk, k4, k2tog, yo], k2.
Row 12: K2, p8, [p1 tbl, p7], k2.

Chart B

Pattern repeat is in [ ].

Row 1 (RS): K2, [yo, ssk, k4, k2tog, (yo) 2 times, ssk, k4, k2tog, yo], k2.
Row 2 (WS): K2, p8, p1 tbl, p7, [(p1 tbl, p7) 2 times], k2.
Row 3: K2, [k4, (k2tog, (yo) 2 times, ssk) 2 times, k4], k2.
Row 4: K2, [p6, p1 tbl, p3, p1 tbl, p5], k2.
Row 5: K2, [k2, k2tog, (yo) 2 times, ssk, k4, k2tog, (yo) 2 times, ssk, k2], k2.
Row 6: K2, [p4, p1 tbl, p7, p1 tbl, p3], k2.
Row 7: K2, [k2tog, (yo) 2 times, ssk, k8, k2tog, (yo) 2 times, ssk], k2.
Row 8: K2, [p2, p1 tbl, p11, p1tbl, p1], k2.
Row 9: K2, [yo, ssk, k4, k2tog, (yo) 2 times, ssk, k4, k2tog, yo], k2.
Row 10: K2, p8, p1 tbl, p7, [(p1 tbl, p7) 2 times], k2.
Row 11: K2, [k4, (k2tog, (yo) 2 times, ssk) 2 times, k4], k2.
Row 12: K2, [p6, p1 tbl, p3, p1 tbl, p5], k2.
Row 13: K2, [k2, k2tog, (yo) 2 times, ssk, k4, k2tog, (yo) 2 times, ssk, k2], k2.
Row 14: K2, [p4, p1 tbl, p7, p1 tbl, p3], k2.
Row 15: K2, [k2tog, (yo) 2 times, ssk, k8, k2tog, (yo) 2 times, ssk], k2.
Row 16: K2, [p2, p1 tbl, p11, p1 tbl, p1], k2.
Row 17: K2, [yo, ssk, k4, k2tog, (yo) 2 times, ssk, k4, k2tog, yo], k2.
Row 18: K2, p8, p1 tbl, p7, [(p1 tbl, p7) 2 times], k2.

Key

■	purl in first pattern repeat
□	RS:knit WS: purl
○	yo
\	ssk
/	k2tog
Ω	RS: k tbl WS: p tbl
□	pattern repeat
•	RS: purl WS: knit

Chart A

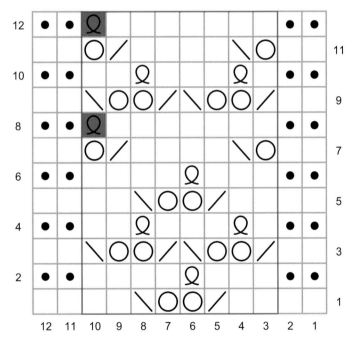

Chart B

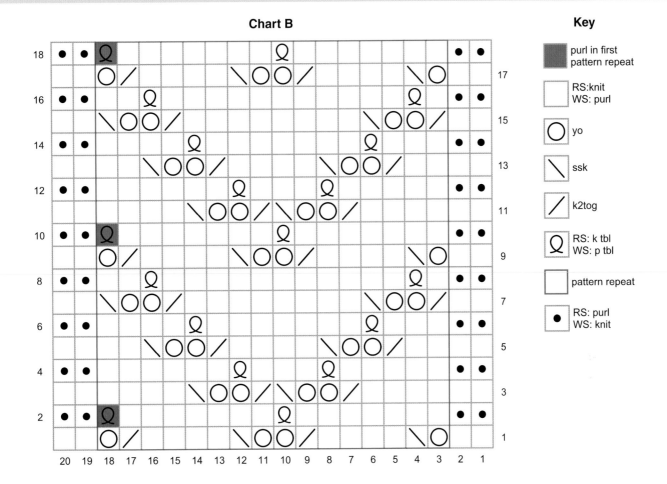

Key

▦	purl in first pattern repeat
☐	RS: knit WS: purl
◯	yo
╲	ssk
╱	k2tog
℧	RS: k tbl WS: p tbl
☐	pattern repeat
•	RS: purl WS: knit

Chart C

Row 1 (RS): K2, [k1, yo, k1, B, k1, ssk, k4, k2tog, k1, B, k1, yo, k1], k2.

Row 2 (WS): K2, [p16], k2.

Row 3: K2, [k2, yo, k1, B, k1, ssk, k2, k2tog, k1, B, k1, yo, k2], k2.

Row 4: K2, [p16], k2.

Row 5: K2, [k3, yo, k1, B, k1, ssk, k2tog, k1, B, k1, yo, k3], k2.

Row 6: K2, [p16], k2.

Row 7: K2, [yo, ssk, k4, B, k2tog, yo, B, k4, k2tog, yo], k2.

Row 8: K2, p16, [p1 tbl, p15], k2.

Row 9: K2, [k2tog, (yo) 2 times, ssk, k2, B, yo, ssk, B, k2, k2tog, (yo) 2 times, ssk], k2.

Row 10: K2, [p2, p1 tbl, p11, p1 tbl, p1], k2.

Row 11: K2, [yo, ssk, k2tog, (yo) 2 times, ssk, B, k2tog, yo, B, k2tog, (yo) 2 times, ssk, k2tog, yo], k2.

Row 12: K2, p4, p1 tbl, p7, p1 tbl, p3, [p1 tbl, p3, p1 tbl, p7, p1 tbl, p3], k2.

Row 13: K2, [k2tog, (yo) 2 times, ssk, k2, B, yo, ssk, B, k2, k2tog, (yo) 2 times, ssk], k2.

Row 14: K2, [p2, p1 tbl, p11, p1 tbl, p1], k2.

Row 15: K2, [yo, ssk, k3, B, k1, k2tog, yo, k1, B, k3, k2tog, yo], k2.

Row 16: K2, p16, [p1 tbl, p15], k2.

Row 17: K2, [k2, k2tog, k1, B, k1, yo, k2, yo, k1, B, k1, ssk, k2], k2.

Row 18: K2, [p16], k2.

Row 19: K2, [k1, k2tog, k1, B, k1, yo, k4, yo, k1, B, k1, ssk, k1], k2.

Row 20: K2, [p16], k2.

Row 21: K2, [k2tog, k1, B, k1, yo, k6, yo, k1, B, k1, ssk], k2.

Row 22: K2, [p16], k2.

Row 23: K2, [k2, k2tog, k1, B, k1, yo, k2, yo, k1, B, k1, ssk, k2], k2.

Row 24: K2, [p16], k2.

Row 25: K2, [k1, k2tog, k1, B, k1, yo, k4, yo, k1, B, k1, ssk, k1], k2.

Row 26: K2, [p16], k2.

Row 27: K2, [k2tog, k1, B, k1, yo, k6, yo, k1, B, k1, ssk], k2.

Row 28: K2, [p16], k2.

Row 29: K1, k2tog, [yo, B, k4, k2tog, (yo) 2 times, ssk, k4, B, k2tog], yo, k1.

Row 30: K2, [p8, p1 tbl, p7], k2.

Row 31: K1, m1, [ssk, B, k2, (k2tog, (yo) 2 times, ssk) 2 times, k2, B, yo], ssk, k1.

(continued)

Key

- purl in first pattern repeat
- RS: knit / WS: purl
- ○ yo
- ＼ ssk
- ／ k2tog
- B add bead and knit st
- ℧ m1
- Ω RS: k tbl / WS: p tbl
- pattern repeat
- • RS: purl / WS: knit

Chart C

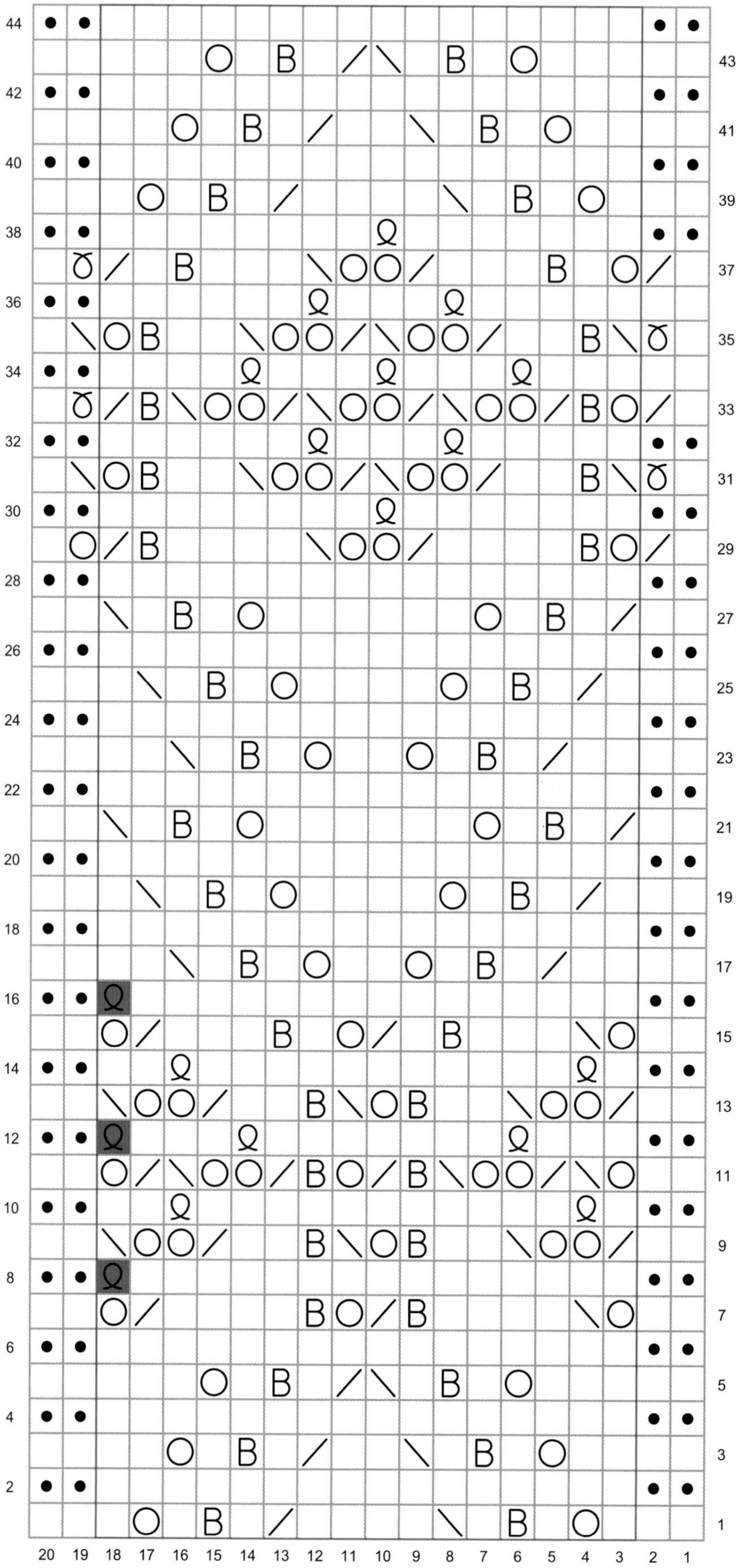

Row 32: K2, [p6, p1 tbl, p3, p1 tbl, p5], k2.

Row 33: K1, k2tog, [yo, B, (k2tog, (yo) 2 times, ssk) 3 times, B, k2tog], m1, k1.

Row 34: K2, [p4, (p1 tbl, p3) 3 times], p2.

Row 35: K1, m1, [ssk, B, k2, (k2tog, (yo) 2 times, ssk) 2 times, k2, B, yo], ssk, k1.

Row 36: K2, [p6, p1 tbl, p3, p1 tbl, p5], p2.

Row 37: K1, k2tog, [yo, k1, B, k3, k2tog, (yo) 2 times, ssk, k3, B, k1, k2tog], m1, k1.

Row 38: K2, [p8, p1 tbl, p7], k2.

Row 39: K2, [k1, yo, k1, B, k1, ssk, k4, k2tog, k1, B, k1, yo, k1], k2.

Row 40: K2, [p16], k2.

Row 41: K2, [k2, yo, k1, B, k1, ssk, k2, k2tog, k1, B, k1, yo, k2], k2.

Row 42: K2, [p16], k2.

Row 43: K2, [k3, yo, k1, B, k1, ssk, k2tog, k1, B, k1, yo, k3], k2.

Row 44: K2, [p16], k2.

Chart D

Pattern repeat is in [ ].

Row 1: K2, [k2, k2tog, yo, k1, B, k2tog, (yo) 4 times, ssk, B, k1, yo, ssk, k2], k2.

Row 2: K2, [p6, B, (p1, p1 tbl) 2 times, B, p6], k2.

Row 3: K2, [k1, k2tog, yo, k1, B, k2tog, yo, k2tog, (yo) 2 times, ssk, yo, ssk, B, k1, yo, ssk, k1], k2.

Row 4: K2, [p5, (B, p1) 2 times, p1 tbl, B, p1, B, p5], k2.

Row 5: K2, [k2tog, yo, k1, B, (k2tog, yo) 2 times, k2, (yo, ssk) 2 times, B, k1, yo, ssk], k2.

Row 6: K2, [(p4, B, p1, B) 2 times, p4], k2.

Row 7: K2, [k2, B, (k2tog, yo) 2 times, k2tog, (yo) 2 times, (ssk, yo) 2 times, ssk, B, k2], k2.

Row 8: K2, [p3, (B, p1) 3 times, p1 tbl, (B, p1) 2 times, B, p3], k2.

Row 9: K2, [k1, B, (k2tog, yo) 3 times, k2, (yo, ssk) 3 times, B, k1], k2.

Row 10: K2, [p2, (B, p1) 2 times, B, p4, (B, p1) 2 times, B, p2], k2.

Key

RS:knit / WS: purl	k2tog	RS: k tbl / WS: p tbl
yo	add bead and knit st	pattern repeat
ssk	add bead and p st	RS: purl / WS: knit

Chart D

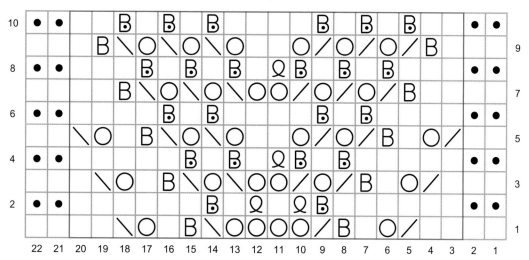

Ariana

This is another design inspired by Elizabeth Zimmerman's pi shawl. In Ariana I've used her formula to create a stunning bead-encrusted shawl with an all-over lace pattern. If the number of beads is too overwhelming, you can add beads to just the edging (Chart D) or to the edging and Chart C.

FINISHED MEASUREMENTS
Width: 68 in./172 cm

YARN
Debbie Bliss Rialto Lace, lace weight #0 yarn, 100% extra-fine superwash merino wool, 426 yd./390 m, 1.75 oz./50 g
- 5 balls #44009 Cyclamen

NEEDLES AND OTHER MATERIALS
- US 3 (3.25 mm) circular needle, 16 in./40 cm and 32 in./80 cm long
- US 3 (3.25 mm) set of double-pointed needles
- 7,104 pale pink size 8 seed beads (debbieabrahamsbeads.co.uk, #39 Shell)
- US 15 (0.50 mm) steel crochet hook (for adding beads)
- Removable stitch marker
- Tapestry needle

GAUGE
16 sts x 32 rows in Chart A patt after blocking = 4 in./10 cm square
Be sure to check your gauge!

Skill Level

Level 3

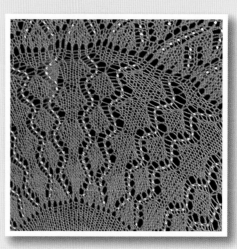

Notes

- This shawl is worked from the center out. Start with dpns and a circular cast-on or the short circular needle and the Disappearing Loop Circular Cast-On; for photo tutorials, see pages 13–17.
- The edging is knitted on sideways at the end.
- For photo tutorials for provisional cast-ons, Russian Bind-Off, and Kitchener Stitch, see pages 7, 17, and 20.
- In Charts A, B, and C, only odd-numbered rounds are charted. Knit even-numbered rounds.

Continue to work in patt through all 12 rows of Chart A for a total of 4 times.

Next 2 rnds: K to end.

Next rnd: (K1, yo) to end—192 sts inc'd, 384 sts.

Next 3 rnds: K to end.

Work Chart B

Rnd 1: Work Row 1 of Chart B 32 times to end.

Rnd 2 and all even-numbered rnds: K to end.

Continue to work in patt through Row 11 of Chart B

Rnd 12: K to 1 st before end of rnd, move marker.

Work Chart C

NOTE: On every even-numbered rnd, stop 1 st before end of rnd and move marker to start next rnd there.

Rnd 1: Work Row 1 of Chart C 32 times to end.

Rnd 2 and all even-numbered rnds: K to end.

Continue to work in patt through all 12 rows of Chart C for a total of 7 times.

Next 2 rnds: K to end.

Next rnd: (K1, yo) to end—384 sts inc'd, 768 sts.

Next 3 rnds: K to end.

Next rnd: Work Row 1 of Chart C 64 times to end.

Next rnd: K to end.

Continue to work in patt through all 12 rows of Chart C for a total of 8 times.

Leave sts on circular needle. Do not bind off.

Edging

NOTE: Edging is worked in garter stitch.

Using a dpn and a provisional cast on, CO 7 sts.

Knit one row.

Row 1 (RS): Work Row 1 of Chart D, knitting the last st of edging tog with 1 st of main shawl (single join; make sure RS of main shawl is facing).

Row 2 (WS): Work Row 2 of Chart D.

Row 3: Work Row 3 of Chart D, knitting the last st of edging tog with the next st of main shawl (single join).

Row 4: Work Row 4 of Chart D.

Continue to work in patt through Chart D a total of 192 times until all sts of the main shawl have been incorporated.

Undo provisional cast-on and place 7 sts from cast-on edge back on a dpn and graft sts tog using Kitchener stitch.

Finishing

Weave in loose ends. Block shawl.

Center of Shawl

Using a circular cast-on method, CO 6 sts. Divide sts evenly between 3 dpns, being careful not to twist them. Join to work in the round. Place a stitch marker to mark beg of rnd.

Rnd 1: K to end.

Rnds 2, 4, and 6: K to end.

Rnd 3: (K1, yo) to end—6 sts inc'd, 12 sts.

Rnd 5: K to end.

Rnd 7: (K1, yo) to end—12 sts inc'd, 24 sts.

Rnds 8–12: K to end.

Rnd 13: (K1, yo) to end—24 sts inc'd, 48 sts.

Rnds 14–24: K to end.

Rnd 25: (K1, yo) to end—48 sts inc'd, 96 sts.

Rnds 26–46: K to end.

Rnd 47: (K1, yo) to end—96 sts inc'd, 192 sts.

Rnds 48–50: K to end.

Work Chart A

Rnd 1: Work Row 1 of Chart A 16 times to end.

Rnd 2 and all even-numbered rnds: K to end.

Chart A

Row 1: K1, yo, B, ssk, k3, k2tog, B, yo, k2.
Row 3: K2, yo, B, ssk, k1, k2tog, B, yo, k3.
Row 5: K3, yo, B, sl1, k2tog, psso, B, yo, k4.
Row 7: K2, k2tog, B, yo, k1, yo, B, ssk, k3.
Row 9: K1, k2tog, B, yo, k3, yo, B, ssk, k2.
Row 11: K2tog, B, yo, k5, yo, B, ssk, k1.

Chart B

Row 1: K2tog, B, (k1, yo) 2 times, k1, B, ssk, k3.
Row 3: B, k1, yo, k3, yo, k1, B, ssk, k1, k2tog.
Row 5: K1, yo, k5, yo, k1, B, sl1, k2tog, psso, B.

Row 7: (Yo, k1) 2 times, B, ssk, k3, k2tog, B, k1.
Row 9: K3, yo, k1, B, ssk, k1, k2tog, B, k1, yo.
Row 11: K4, yo, k1, B, sl1, k2tog, psso, B, k1, yo, k1.

Chart C

Row 1: K2tog, B, (k1, yo) 2 times, k1, B, ssk, k3.
Row 3: K2tog, B, k1, yo, k3, yo, k1, B, ssk, k1.
Row 5: Sl1, k2tog, psso, B, k1, yo, k5, yo, k1, B.
Row 7: K2tog, B, k1 (yo, k1) 2 times, B, ssk, k3.
Row 9: K2tog, B, k1, yo, k3, yo, k1, B, ssk, k1.
Row 11: Sl1, k2tog, psso, B, k1, yo, k5, yo, k1, B.

Key

☐	knit
◯	yo
╱	k2tog
╲	ssk
∧	sl1, k2tog, psso
B	add bead and knit

Chart A

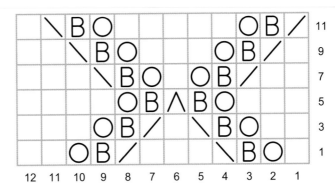

Chart B

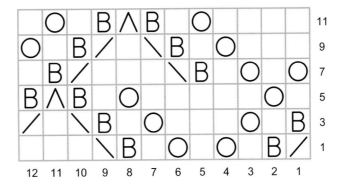

Chart C

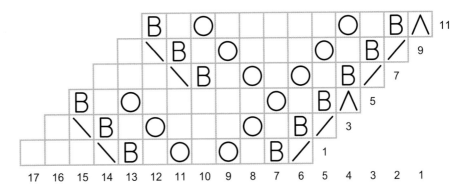

Chart D

Row 1 (RS): Sl wyif, k1, (yo) 3 times, k1, k2tog, yo, k1, SJ.
Row 2 (WS): Sl wyif, k2tog, yo, k2, B dropping extra loops, k2.
Row 3: Sl wyif, k1, (yo) 3 times, k2, k2tog, yo, k1, SJ.
Row 4: Sl wyif, k2tog, yo, k3, B dropping extra loops, k2.
Row 5: Sl wyif, k1, (yo) 3 times, k3, k2tog, yo, k1, SJ.
Row 6: Sl wyif, k2tog, yo, k4, B dropping extra loops, k2.
Row 7: RBO 3, k2, k2tog, yo, k1, SJ.
Row 8: Sl wyif, k2tog, yo, k4.

Key

knit

yo

k2tog

add bead and drop extra loops

single join

Russian bind-off

slip purlwise with yarn in front

st left from RBO

yo 3 times

Chart D

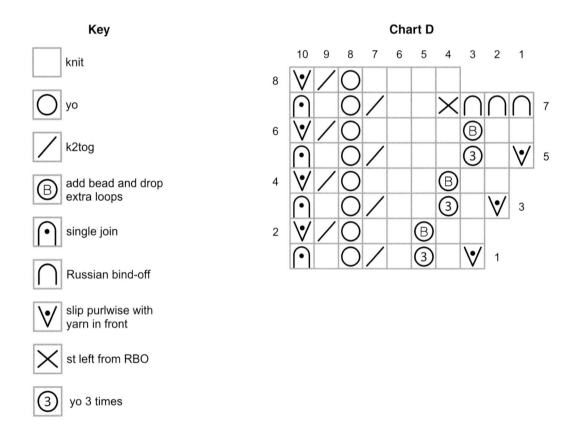

Josephine

This crescent shawl starts with a wide beaded border with lace patterning on both right and wrong side rows. The tapered shape is achieved by working a combination of short rows and decreases in stockinette stitch, with beads scattered throughout.

Skill Level

Level 3

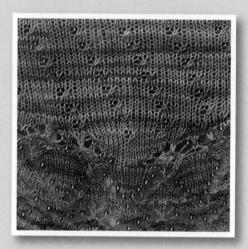

Notes

- Josephine is shaped by working short rows and decreases on every row. On the first two rows you work partway across the row, leaving a number of stitches unworked when you turn. Turning will create a visible gap. On subsequent rows you work until 1 stitch before the gap, then work a decrease across the gap (including 1 stitch from either side of the gap). After the decrease, knit/purl 3, then turn again. You're gradually working back and forth across the stitches you left unworked on Rows 1 and 2. On Row 3 there is a pattern repeat that adds beads. The first time you work Row 3, this pattern repeat is worked once. The next time you work Row 3, you work the pattern repeat 4 times.

FINISHED MEASUREMENTS

Small (Large)
Inner crescent: 27$\frac{1}{2}$ (47) in./70 (119.5) cm
Outer crescent: 52$\frac{1}{2}$ (81) in./133.5 (205.5) cm
Depth: 14 (16) in./35.5 (40.5) cm

YARN

Malabrigo Lace, lace weight #0 yarn, 100% baby merino wool, 470 yd./430 m, 1.75 oz./50 g
- 1 (1) skein #37 Lettuce

NEEDLES AND OTHER MATERIALS

- US 4 (3.5 mm) circular needle, 32 in./80 cm long
- 780 (810) size 8 lime green seed beads (debbieabrahamsbeads.co.uk, #48 Lime)
- US 15 (0.50 mm) steel crochet hook (for adding beads)
- Stitch markers
- Tapestry needle

GAUGE

20 sts x 28.5 rows in Chart patt after blocking = 4 in./10 cm square
Be sure to check your gauge!

Cast On

CO 269 (341) sts using Long-Tail Cast-On over two needles or another very stretchy cast-on.

Rows 1–3: Knit.

Work Chart A

Row 1 (RS): Work Row 1 of Chart A, working patt rep 11 (14) times.

Row 2 (WS): Work Row 2 of Chart A, working patt rep 11(14) times.

Continue to work in patt through all 40 rows of Chart A once.

Short-Row Section

Working in stockinette stitch short rows (without wrapping the sts), continue as follows:

Row 1 (RS): K141 (177), turn—128 (164) sts remain unworked.

Row 2 (WS): P13 (13), turn—128 (164) sts remain unworked.

Row 3: Sl, k2, [k2, k2tog, (yo) 3 times, k3], k to 1 st before last turning point, ssk, k3, turn—1 st dec'd.

Row 4: Sl wyif, p to triple yo, drop 2 yo's, add bead and purl st, p to 1 st before last turning point, p2tog, p3, turn—1 st dec'd.

Row 5: Sl, k to 1 st before last turning point, ssk, k3, turn—1 st dec'd.

Row 6: Sl wyif, p to 1 st before last turning point, p2tog, p3, turn—1 st dec'd.

Rep Rows 3–6, repeating the patt rep on Row 3 in brackets additional times on each row until all remaining unworked sts have been worked—205 (259) sts.

BO all sts.

Finishing

Weave in loose ends. Block shawl.

Chart A

Pattern repeat is in [ ].

Row 1 (RS): Sl wyif, k2, [(k5, yo, k5, k2tog) 2 times], k2.

Rows 2, 4, 6, 8, 10, 12, 14, and 16: Sl wyif, k1, p to last 2 sts, k2.

Row 3: Sl wyif, k1, k2tog, [(k4, yo, B, yo, k4, sl1, k2tog, psso) 2 times], rep to last 26 sts, k4, yo, B, yo, k4, sl1, k2tog, psso, k4, yo, B, yo, k4, k2tog, k2.

Row 5: Sl wyif, k1, k2tog, [(k3, yo, B, k1, B, yo, k3, sl1, k2tog, psso) 2 times], rep to last 26 sts, k3, yo, B, k1, B, yo, k3, sl1, k2tog, psso, k3, yo, B, k1, B, yo, k3, k2tog, k2.

Row 7: Sl wyif, k1, k2tog, [(k2, yo, k2tog, yo, B, yo, ssk, yo, k2, sl1, k2tog, psso) 2 times], rep to last 26 sts, k2, yo, k2tog, yo, B, yo, ssk, yo, k2, sl1, k2tog, psso, k2, yo, k2tog, yo, B, yo, ssk, yo, k2, k2tog, k2.

Row 9: Sl wyif, k1, k2tog, [(k1, yo, k2tog, yo, B, k1, B, yo, ssk, yo, k1, sl1, k2tog, psso) 2 times], rep to last 26 sts, k1, yo, k2tog, yo, B, k1, B, yo, ssk, yo, k1, sl1, k2tog, psso, k1, yo, k2tog, yo, B, k1, B, yo, ssk, yo, k1, k2tog, k2.

Row 11: Sl wyif, k1, k2tog, [(yo, k3, yo, sl1, k2tog, psso) 4 times], rep to last 26 sts, (yo, k3, yo, sl1, k2tog, psso) 3 times, yo, k3, yo, k2tog, k2.

Row 13: Sl wyif, k2, [k1, (yo, sl1, k2tog, psso, yo, k3) 3 times, yo, sl1, k2tog, psso, yo, k2], k2.

Row 15: Sl wyif, k2, [k3, k2tog, yo, B, yo, ssk, k7, k2tog, yo, B, yo, ssk, k4], k2.

Row 17: Sl wyif, k1, B, [(yo, ssk, k2tog, yo, B, k1, B, yo, ssk, k2tog, yo, B) 2 times], k2.

Row 18: Sl wyif, k1, [p2, yo, p2tog, p5, ssp, yo, p3, yo, p2tog, p5, ssp, yo, p1], p1, k2.

Row 19: Sl wyif, k2, [k1, B, yo, sl1, k2tog, psso, yo, k1, yo, sl1, k2tog, psso, yo, B, k3, B, yo, sl1, k2tog, psso, yo, k1, yo, sl1, k2tog, psso, yo, B, k2], k2.

Row 20: Sl wyif, k1, [p4, yo, p2tog, p1, ssp, yo, p7, yo, p2tog, p1, ssp, yo, p3], p1, k2.

(continued)

Row 21: Sl wyif, k2, [k3, B, yo, sl1, k2tog, psso, yo, B, k7, B, yo, sl1, k2tog, psso, yo, B, k4], k2.

Rows 22, 24, 26, 28, 30, and 32: Sl wyif, k1, p to last 2 sts, k2.

Row 23: Sl wyif, k1, B, [(yo, ssk, k1, k2tog, yo, k1, yo, ssk, k1, k2tog, yo, B) 2 times], k2.

Row 25: Sl wyif, k2, [(B, yo, ssk, k5, k2tog, yo, B, k1) 2 times], k2.

Row 27: Sl wyif, k2, [k1, B, yo, ssk, k3, k2tog, yo, B, k3, B, yo, ssk, k3, k2tog, yo, B, k2], k2.

Row 29: Sl wyif, k2, [k2, B, yo, ssk, k1, k2tog, yo, B, k5, B, yo, ssk, k1, k2tog, yo, B, k3], k2.

Row 31: Sl wyif, k2, [k3, B, yo, sl1, k2tog, psso, yo, B, k7, B, yo, sl1, k2tog, psso, yo, B, k4], k2.

Row 33: Sl wyif, k2, [k5, yo, ssk, k9, k2tog, yo, k6], k2.

Row 34: Sl wyif, k1, [p3, yo, p4, p2tog, p7, ssp, p4, yo, p2], p1, k2.

Row 35: Sl wyif, k2, [k2, B, yo, k4, ssk, k5, k2tog, k4, yo, B, k3], k2.

Row 36: Sl wyif, k1, [p5, yo, p4, p2tog, p3, ssp, p4, yo, p4], p1, k2.

Row 37: Sl wyif, k2, [k4, B, yo, k4, ssk, B, k2tog, k4, yo, B, k5], k2.

Row 38: Sl wyif, k1, [p7, yo, p2tog, p1, ssp, yo, p1, yo, p2tog, p1, ssp, yo, p6], p1, k2.

Row 39: Sl wyif, k2, [k6, B, yo, sl1, k2tog, psso, yo, B, k1, B, yo, sl1, k2tog, psso, yo, B, k7], k2.

Row 40: Sl wyif, k1, p to last 2 sts, k2.

The smaller version of Josephine

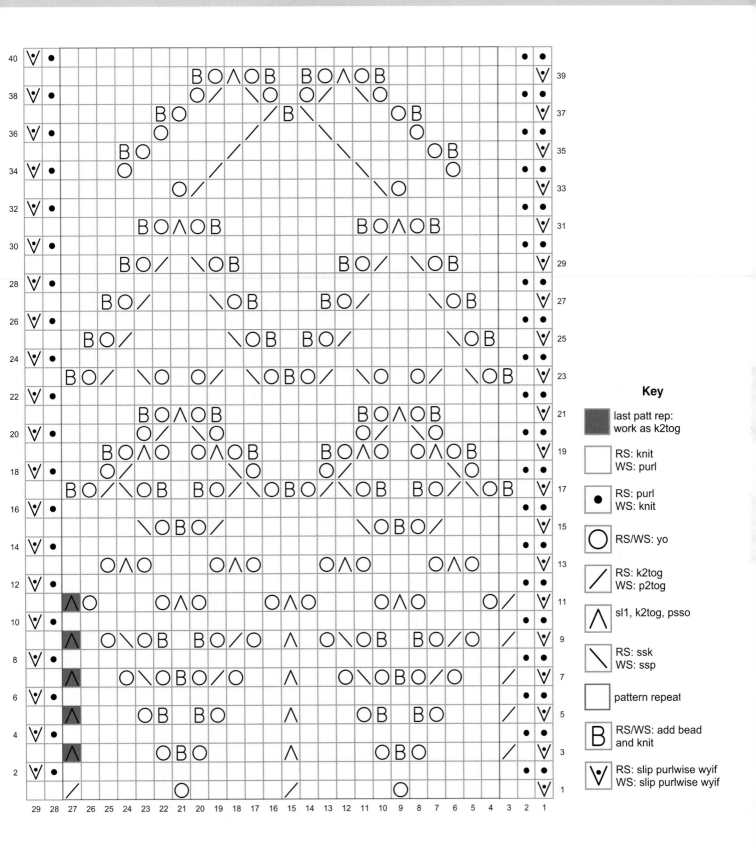

Key

last patt rep:
work as k2tog

RS: knit
WS: purl

● RS: purl
WS: knit

○ RS/WS: yo

/ RS: k2tog
WS: p2tog

∧ sl1, k2tog, psso

\ RS: ssk
WS: ssp

pattern repeat

B RS/WS: add bead
and knit

V RS: slip purlwise wyif
WS: slip purlwise wyif

Cerina

This shawl will be worked from the top down with a center insertion that creates a slightly rounded shape. The shawl starts with a small lace pattern, then transitions to a larger lace pattern and finishes with a scalloped edging.

FINISHED MEASUREMENTS

Width: 71$^1/_2$ in./182 cm
Depth (center back): 31$^1/_2$ in./80 cm

YARN

Manos del Uruguay Lace, lace weight #0 yarn, 70% baby alpaca/25% silk/5% cashmere, 439 yd./400 m, 1.75 oz./50 g
- 1 skein #2458 Breena

NEEDLES AND OTHER MATERIALS

- US 4 (3.5 mm) circular needle (32 in./80 cm long)
- 1,266 blue size 8 seed beads (thebeadroom.co.uk, #633)
- US steel 15 (0.50 mm) crochet hook (for adding beads)
- Tapestry needle

GAUGE

15.5 sts x 24 rows in Chart E patt after blocking = 4 in./10 cm square
Be sure to check your gauge!

Skill Level

Level 3

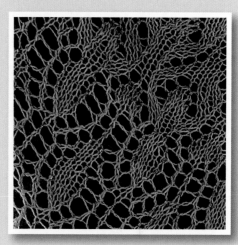

Notes

- All charts show RS rows only. See pattern for WS rows.
- See page 17 for a photo tutorial of Russian Bind-Off.

Work Charts A and E

Row 1: K2, work Row 11 of Chart A, work Row 1 of Chart E, work Row 11 of Chart A, k2—4 sts inc'd.

Row 2 and all WS rows: K2, p to last 2 sts, k2.

Row 3: K2, work Row 13 of Chart A, work Row 3 of Chart E, work Row 13 of Chart A, k2—4 sts inc'd.

Continue to work in patt through all 34 rows of Chart A once and all 12 rows of Chart E a total of 2 times—91 sts.

Work Charts B and E

Row 1 (RS): K2, work Row 1 of Chart B working patt rep once, work Row 1 of Chart E, work Row 1 of Chart B working patt rep once, k2—4 sts inc'd.

Row 2 and all WS rows: K2, p to last 2 sts, k2.

Row 3: K2, work Row 3 of Chart B working patt rep once, work Row 31 of Chart E, work Row 3 of Chart B working patt rep once, k2—4 sts inc'd.

Continue to work in patt through all 12 rows of Chart B and Chart E a total of 6 times. Each time Chart B is repeated, work the patt rep one additional time for each row—235 sts.

Work Charts C and E

Row 1 (RS): K2, work Row 1 of Chart C working patt rep 7 times, work Row 1 of Chart E, work Row 1 of Chart C working patt rep 7 times, k2—4 sts inc'd.

Row 2 and all WS rows: K2, p to last 2 sts, k2.

Row 3: K2, work Row 3 of Chart C working patt rep 7 times, work Row 3 of Chart E, work Row 3 of Chart C working patt rep 7 times, k2—4 sts inc'd.

Continue to work in patt through all 12 rows of Chart C and Chart E a total of 6 times. Each time Chart C is repeated, work the patt rep one additional time for each row—379 sts.

Cast On

CO 23 sts.

Knit one row.

Work Chart A

Row 1 (RS): K2, work Row 1 of Chart A, k17, work Row 1 of Chart A, k2—4 sts inc'd.

Row 2 and all WS rows: K2, p to last 2 sts, k2.

Row 3: K2, work Row 3 of Chart A, k17, work Row 3 of Chart A, k2—4 sts inc'd.

Continue to work in patt through Row 10 of Chart A—43 sts.

Work Charts D and E

Row 1 (RS): K2, work Row 1 of Chart D working patt rep 13 times, work Row 1 of Chart E, work Row 1 of Chart D working patt rep 13 times, k2—4 sts inc'd.

Row 2 and all WS rows: K2, p to last 2 sts, k2.

Row 3 (RS): K2, work Row 3 of Chart D working patt rep 13 times, work Row 3 of Chart E, work Row 3 of Chart D working patt rep 13 times, k2—4 sts inc'd.

Continue to work in patt through all 12 rows of Chart D and Chart E once—403 sts.

BO using Russian Bind-Off.

Finishing

Weave in loose ends. Block shawl.

Chart A

Row 1 (RS): Yo, k1, yo.
Row 3: Yo, k3, yo.
Row 5: Yo, k5, yo.
Row 7: Yo, k7, yo.
Row 9: Yo, k9, yo.
Row 11: Yo, ssk, k3, yo, B, yo, k3, k2tog, yo.
Row 13: Yo, k1, ssk, k2, yo, B, k1, B, yo, k2, k2tog, k1, yo.
Row 15: Yo, k2, ssk, k1, yo, B, k3, B, yo, k1, k2tog, k2, yo.
Row 17: Yo, k2, B, yo, k3, k2tog, k1, ssk, k3, yo, B, k2, yo.
Row 19: Yo, k4, B, yo, k2, k2tog, k1, ssk, k2, yo, B, k4, yo.
Row 21: Yo, k6, B, yo, k1, k2tog, k1, ssk, k1, yo, B, k6, yo.
Row 23: Yo, ssk, k3, yo, B, yo, k3, k2tog, k1, ssk, k3, yo, B, yo, k3, k2tog, yo.
Row 25: Yo, (k1, ssk, k2, yo, B, k1, B, yo, k2, k2tog) 2 times, k1, yo.

Row 27: Yo, k2, ssk, k1, yo, B, k3, B, yo, k1, k2tog, k1, ssk, k1, yo, B, k3, B, yo, k1, k2tog, k2, yo.
Row 29: Yo, k2, (B, yo, k3, k2tog, k1, ssk, k3, yo) 2 times, B, k2, yo.
Row 31: Yo, k4, B, yo, k2, k2tog, k1, ssk, k2, yo, B, k1, B, yo, k2, k2tog, k1, ssk, k2, yo, B, k4, yo.
Row 33: Yo, k6, B, yo, k1, k2tog, k1, ssk, k1, yo, B, k3, B, yo, k1, k2tog, k1, ssk, k1, yo, B, k6, yo.

Chart B

Pattern repeat is in [ ].

Row 1 (RS): Yo, ssk, k3, yo, B, yo, k3, k2tog, [k1, ssk, k3, yo, B, yo, k3, k2tog], k1, ssk, k3, yo, B, yo, k3, k2tog, yo.
Row 3: Yo, k1, ssk, k2, yo, B, k1, B, yo, k2, k2tog, [k1, ssk, k2, yo, B, k1, B, yo, k2, k2tog], k1, ssk, k2, yo, B, k1, B, yo, k2, k2tog, k1, yo.
Row 5: Yo, k2, ssk, k1, yo, B, k3, B, yo, k1, k2tog, [k1, ssk, k1, yo, B, k3, B, yo, k1, k2tog], k1, ssk, k1, yo, B, k3, B, yo, k1, k2tog, k2, yo.

(continued)

Chart A

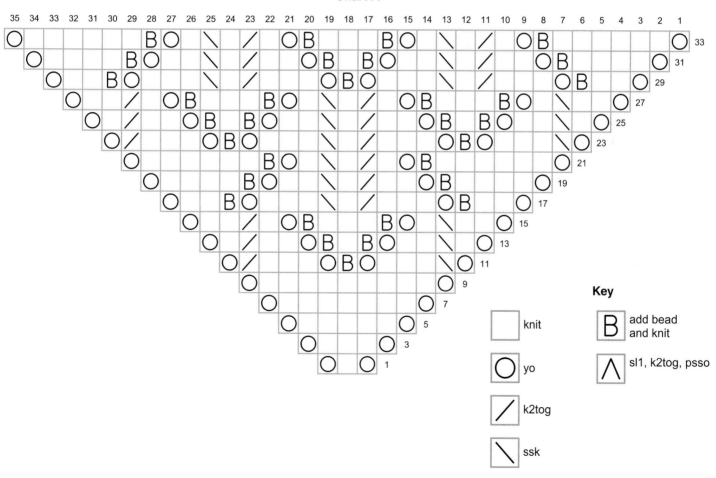

Key

☐	knit
◯	yo
╱	k2tog
╲	ssk
B	add bead and knit
∧	sl1, k2tog, psso

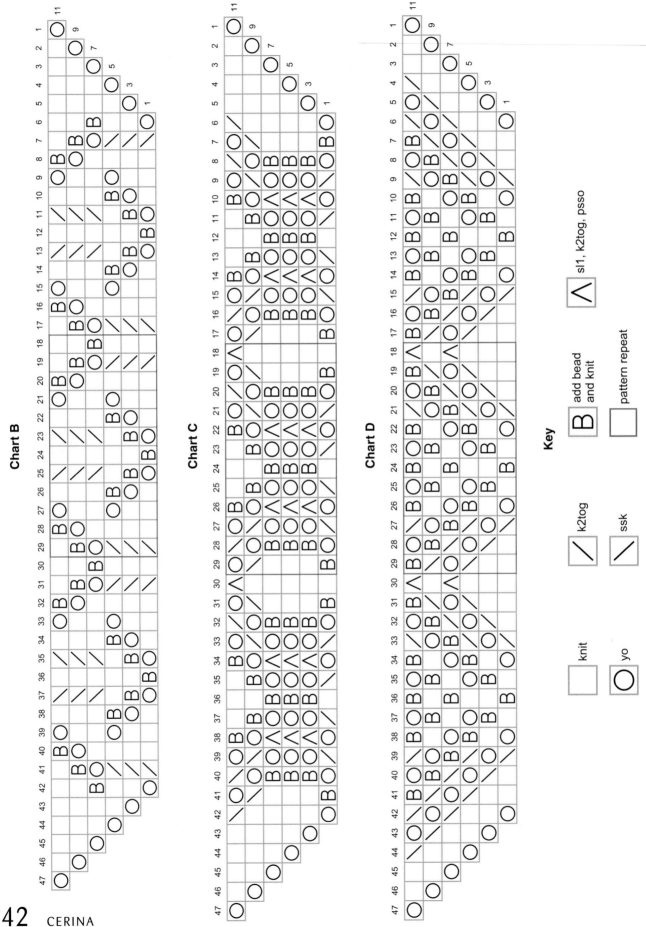

Chart B

Chart C

Chart D

Key

	knit			k2tog			sl1, k2tog, psso
○	yo		/	ssk		B	add bead and knit
							pattern repeat

Row 7: Yo, k2, B, yo, k3, k2tog, k1, ssk, k3, yo, [B, yo, k3, k2tog, k1, ssk, k3, yo], B, yo, k3, k2tog, k1, ssk, k3, yo, B, k2, yo.

Row 9: Yo, k4, B, yo, k2, k2tog, k1, ssk, k2, yo, B, [k1, B, yo, k2, k2tog, k1, ssk, k2, yo, B], k1, B, yo, k2, k2tog, k1, ssk, k2, yo, B, k4, yo.

Row 11: Yo, k6, B, yo, k1, k2tog, k1, ssk, k1, yo, B, k1, [k2, B, yo, k1, k2tog, k1, ssk, k1, yo, B, k1], k2, B, yo, k1, k2tog, k1, ssk, k1, yo, B, k6, yo.

Chart C

Pattern repeat is in [ ].

Row 1 (RS): Yo, B, (yo, ssk) 2 times, k1, (k2tog, yo) 2 times, B, [k1, B, (yo, ssk) 2 times, k1, (k2tog, yo) 2 times, B], k1, B, (yo, ssk) 2 times, k1, (k2tog, yo) 2 times, B, yo.

Row 3: Yo, k2, (B, yo, sl1, k2tog, psso, yo) 2 times, B, k1, [k2, (B, yo, sl1, k2tog, psso, yo) 2 times, B, k1], k2, (B, yo, sl1, k2tog, psso, yo) 2 times, B, k2, yo.

Row 5: Yo, k3, (B, yo, sl1, k2tog, psso, yo) 2 times, B, k1, [k2, (B, yo, sl1, k2tog, psso, yo) 2 times, B, k1], k2, (B, yo, sl1, k2tog, psso, yo) 2 times, B, k3, yo.

Row 7: Yo, k4, (B, yo, sl1, k2tog, psso, yo) 2 times, B, k1, [k2, (B, yo, sl1, k2tog, psso, yo) 2 times, B, k1], k2, (B, yo, sl1, k2tog, psso, yo) 2 times, B, k4, yo.

Row 9: Yo, k4, (k2tog, yo) 2 times, B, k1, B, (yo, ssk) 2 times, [k1, (k2tog, yo) 2 times, B, k1, B, (yo, ssk) 2 times], k1, (k2tog, yo) 2 times, B, k1, B, (yo, ssk) 2 times, k4, yo.

Row 11: Yo, k4, (k2tog, yo) 2 times, B, k3, B, yo, ssk, yo, [sl1, k2tog, psso, yo, k2tog, yo, B, k3, B, yo, ssk, yo], sl1, k2tog, psso, yo, k2tog, yo, B, k3, B, (yo, ssk) 2 times, k4, yo.

Chart D

Pattern repeat is in [ ].

Row 1 (RS): Yo, k2, k2tog, yo, k1, B, k1, yo, ssk, k2, [k3, k2tog, yo, k1, B, k1, yo, ssk, k2], k3, k2tog, yo, k1, B, k1, yo, ssk, k2, yo.

Row 3: Yo, k2, k2tog, yo, (k1, B) 2 times, k1, yo, ssk, k1, [k2, k2tog, yo, (k1, B) 2 times, k1, yo, ssk, k1], k2, k2tog, yo, (k1, B) 2 times, k1, yo, ssk, k2, yo.

Row 5: Yo, k2, k2tog, yo, k2tog, B, yo, k1, yo, B, ssk, yo, ssk, [k1, k2tog, yo, k2tog, B, yo, k1, yo, B, ssk, yo, ssk], k1, k2tog, yo, k2tog, B, yo, k1, yo, B, ssk, yo, ssk, k2, yo.

Row 7: Yo, k2, k2tog, yo, k2tog, B, yo, k1, B, k1, yo, B, ssk, yo, [sl1, k2tog, psso, yo, k2tog, B, yo, k1, B, k1, yo, B, ssk, yo], sl1, k2tog, psso, yo, k2tog, B, yo, k1, B, k1, yo, B, ssk, yo, ssk, k2, yo.

Row 9: Yo, k2, k2tog, yo, k2tog, B, yo, (k1, B) 2 times, k1, yo, B, ssk, [k1, k2tog, B, yo, (k1, B) 2 times, k1, yo, B, ssk], k1, k2tog, B, yo, (k1, B) 2 times, k1, yo, B, ssk, yo, ssk, k2, yo.

Row 11: Yo, k2, k2tog, (yo, k2tog, B) 2 times, (yo, B) 2 times, ssk, yo, B, [sl1, k2tog, psso, B, yo, k2tog, (B, yo) 2 times, B, ssk, yo, B], sl1, k2tog, psso, B, yo, k2tog, B, yo, B, (yo, B, ssk) 2 times, yo, ssk, k2, yo.

Chart E

Row 1: K5, k2tog, yo, k3, yo, ssk, k5.

Row 3: K4, k2tog, yo, k2, B, k2, yo, ssk, k4.

Row 5: K3, k2tog, yo, k2, B, k1, B, k2, yo, ssk, k3.

Row 7: K2, k2tog, yo, B, yo, ssk, k1, B, k1, k2tog, yo, B, yo, ssk, k2.

Row 9: (K1, k2tog, yo, B, k1, B, yo, ssk) 2 times, k1.

Row 11: K2tog, yo, B, k3, B, yo, sl1, k2tog, psso, yo, B, k3, B, yo, ssk.

Chart E

Key

☐	knit
○	yo
╱	k2tog
╲	ssk
B	add bead and knit
⋀	sl1, k2tog, psso

Tamar

The beaded central panel of this rectangular stole is knit first, then wide borders are knitted onto it at either end.

Level 3

FINISHED MEASUREMENTS
Width: 21 in./53.5 cm
Length: 56 in./142 cm

YARN
Plymouth Yarn Baby Alpaca Lace, lace weight #0 yarn, 100% baby alpaca, 437 yd./400 m, 1.75 oz./50 g
- 2 skeins #0402 Gray

NEEDLES AND OTHER MATERIALS
- US 4 (3.5 mm) straight or circular needles
- 1,192 metallic silver size 8 seed beads (debbieabrahamsbeads.co.uk, #563 Metallic Silver)
- US 15 (0.50 mm) steel crochet hook (for adding beads)
- Waste yarn
- Stitch holder (optional)
- Tapestry needle

GAUGE
16 sts x 30 rows in Chart A patt after blocking = 4 in./10 cm square
Be sure to check your gauge!

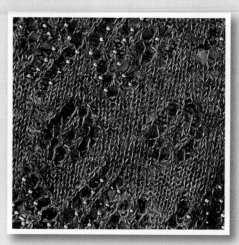

Notes

- This shawl begins with a provisional cast-on (any method is fine); for photo tutorials, see page 7–11.
- In Chart A, only RS rows are shown. See pattern for WS rows.
- See page 17 for a photo tutorial for Russian Bind-Off.

Row 1: Work Row 1 of Chart B, k last st of Chart B tog with one st from Center Panel (Single Join).

Continue to work in patt through all 10 rows of Chart B a total of 17 times.

BO using Russian Bind-Off.

Pull out provisional CO from the other side of the Center Panel and place the live sts on a needle—85 sts.

Work Edging again as above.

Finishing

Weave in loose ends. Block shawl.

Chart A

Pattern repeat is in [ ].

Row 1 (RS): Sl wyif, k2, [k8, yo, ssk, k7, k2tog, yo, k7], k4.

Row 3: Sl wyif, k2, [k6, yo, ssk, B, yo, ssk, k5, k2tog, yo, B, k2tog, yo, k5], k4.

Row 5: Sl wyif, k2, [k6, (B, yo, ssk) 2 times, k3, (k2tog, yo, B) 2 times, k5], k4.

Row 7: Sl wyif, k2, [k3, yo, sl1, k2tog, psso, yo, k1, (B, yo, ssk) 2 times, k1, (k2tog, yo, B) 2 times, k1, yo, sl1, k2tog, psso, yo, k2], k4.

Row 9: Sl wyif, k2, [k1, k2tog, yo, k1, B, k1, (yo, ssk, B) 2 times, yo, sl1, k2tog, psso, (yo, B, k2tog) 2 times, yo, k1, B, k1, yo, ssk], k4.

Row 11: Sl wyif, k2, [k3, yo, sl1, k2tog, psso, yo, k1, (k2tog, yo, B) 2 times, k1, (B, yo, ssk) 2 times, k1, yo, sl1, k2tog, psso, yo, k2], k4.

Row 13: Sl wyif, k2, [k6, (k2tog, yo, B) 2 times, k3, (B, yo, ssk) 2 times, k5], k4.

Row 15: Sl wyif, k2, [k5, (k2tog, yo, B) 2 times, k5, (B, yo, ssk) 2 times, k4], k4.

Row 17: Sl wyif, k2, [k6, B, k2tog, yo, B, k7, B, yo, ssk, B, k5], k4.

Row 19: Sl wyif, k to end.

Row 21: Sl wyif, k2, [(k1, yo, ssk, k8, k2tog, yo) 2 times], k4.

Row 23: Sl wyif, k2, [k2, yo, ssk, k6, k2tog, yo, k3, yo, ssk, k6, k2tog, yo, k1], k4.

Row 25: Sl wyif, k1, k2tog, [(yo, k2, yo, ssk, k4, k2tog, yo, k1, k2tog) 2 times], yo, k3.

Row 27: Sl wyif, k2, [k1, k2tog, yo, k8, yo, ssk, k1, k2tog, yo, k8, yo, ssk], k4.

Row 29: Sl wyif, k2, k2tog, yo, k10, yo, sl1, k2tog, psso, yo, k10, yo [sl1, k2tog, psso, yo, k10, yo, sl1, k2tog, psso, yo, k10, yo], ssk, k3.

Row 31: Sl wyif, k to end.

Chart B

Row 1 (RS): Sl wyif, B, (yo, k2tog) 6 times, yo, k1, SJ.

Row 2 (WS): Sl wyif, k2tog, yo, k14.

Center Panel

Using a provisional cast-on, CO 86 sts.

Purl one row, p2tog in center of row—85 sts.

Row 1 (RS): Work Row 1 of Chart A, working patt rep 3 times.

Row 2 and all WS rows: Sl wyif, k2, p to last 3 sts, k3.

Continue to work in patt through all 32 rows of Chart A a total of 11 times.

Do not bind off. Leave sts on needle.

Edging

CO 16 sts to a spare needle.

Knit one row.

The last st of every other row of the edging will be knit tog with one st from the Center Panel with the RS facing (Single Join).

Row 3: Sl wyif, B, (yo, k2tog) 5 times, yo, k1, k2tog, yo, k1, SJ.
Row 4: Sl wyif, k2tog, yo, k15.
Row 5: Sl wyif, B, (yo, k2tog) 5 times, yo, k2, k2tog, yo, k1, SJ.
Row 6: Sl wyif, k2tog, yo, k16.
Row 7: Sl wyif, B, (yo, k2tog) 5 times, yo, k3, k2tog, yo, k1, SJ.
Row 8: Sl wyif, k2tog, yo, k17.
Row 9: RBO 4 times, k11, k2tog, yo, k1, SJ.
Row 10: Sl wyif, k2tog, yo, k13.

Key

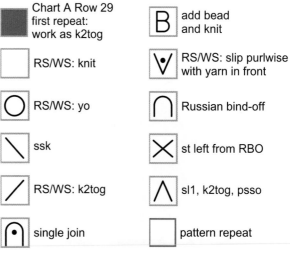

▨	Chart A Row 29 first repeat: work as k2tog
☐	RS/WS: knit
◯	RS/WS: yo
╲	ssk
╱	RS/WS: k2tog
⌂	single join

B	add bead and knit
V	RS/WS: slip purlwise with yarn in front
∩	Russian bind-off
✕	st left from RBO
⋀	sl1, k2tog, psso
☐	pattern repeat

Chart A

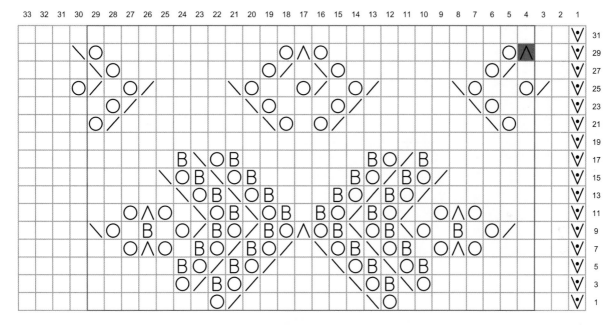

Chart B

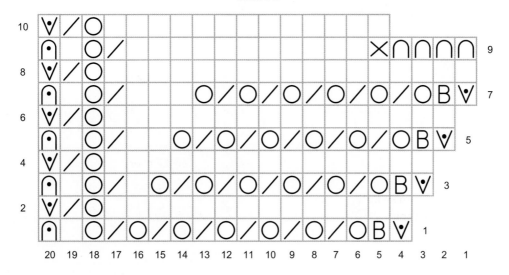

Chatelaine is a beautiful stole with a complex beaded lace pattern. A luxurious merino/silk blend yarn makes this a perfect accessory to dress up any outfit.

FINISHED MEASUREMENTS
Width: 18 in./45 cm
Depth: 60^1/$_2$ in./154 cm

YARN
Juniper Moon Farm Findley, lace weight #1 yarn, 50% merino/50% silk, 798 yd./730 m, 3.5 oz./100 g
- 1 skein #21 Malachite

NEEDLES AND OTHER MATERIALS
- US 4 (3.5 mm) straight needles
- 864 amethyst size 8 seed beads (debbieabrahamsbeads.co.uk, #41 Amethyst)
- US 15 (0.50 mm) steel crochet hook (for adding beads)
- Tapestry needle

GAUGE
18 sts x 26 rows in Lace Pattern after blocking = 4 in./10 cm square
Be sure to check your gauge!

Skill Level
Level 3

Notes

- This scarf is worked flat. You can make it longer by adding more repeats or wider by adding stitches in groups of 24, but you'll need to buy at least another skein of yarn to do that.
- Chart shows RS only; see pattern for WS rows.
- For a photo tutorial of Russian Bind-Off, see page 17.

Finishing

Weave in all loose ends. Block shawl.

Lace Pattern

Pattern repeat is in [ ].

Row 1(RS): Sl wyif, k3, [k4, (yo, ssk) 2 times, k1, k2tog, yo, k3, yo, ssk, k1, (k2tog, yo) 2 times, k3], k5.

Row 2 (WS and all following WS rows): Sl wyif, k1, p to last 2 sts, k2.

Row 3: Sl wyif, k3, [k2, k2tog, yo, k1, yo, ssk, yo, sl1, k2tog, psso, yo, k5, yo, sl1, k2tog, psso, yo, k2tog, yo, k1, yo, ssk, k1], k5.

Row 5: Sl wyif, k3, [k1, k2tog, yo, k3, (yo, ssk) 2 times, k5, (k2tog, yo) 2 times, k3, yo, ssk], k5.

Row 7: Sl wyif, k2, yo, [sl1, k2tog, psso, yo, k2, B, k2, yo, ssk, k1, ssk, yo, k1, yo, k2tog, k1, k2tog, yo, k2, B, k2, yo], sl1, k2tog, psso, yo, k3.

Row 9: Sl wyif, k1, yo, ssk, [(yo, ssk) 2 times, k1, B, k2, yo, ssk, k1, yo, sl1, k2tog, psso, yo, k1, k2tog, yo, k2, B, k1, k2tog, yo, k1], yo, ssk, k3.

Row 11: Sl wyif, k1, k2tog, yo, [k1, (yo, ssk) 2 times, k1, B, k2, yo, sl1, k2tog, psso, yo, k1, yo, sl1, k2tog, psso, yo, k2, B, k1, (k2tog, yo) 2 times], k2tog, yo, k3.

Row 13: Sl wyif, k2, k2tog, [yo, k1, (yo, ssk) 2 times, k1, B, k2, yo, ssk, k1, k2tog, yo, k2, B, k1, (k2tog, yo) 2 times, k2tog], yo, k4.

Row 15: Sl wyif, k2, yo, [sl1, k2tog, psso, yo, k2tog, yo, k1, yo, ssk, k1, B, k2, yo, sl1, k2tog, psso, yo, k2, B, k1, k2tog, yo, k1, yo, ssk, yo], sl1, k2tog, psso, yo, k3.

Row 17: Sl wyif, k3, [yo, sl1, k2tog, psso, yo, k2tog, yo, k2, B, k1, k2tog, yo, k3, yo, ssk, k1, B, k2, (yo, ssk) 2 times], yo, ssk, k3.

Row 19: Sl wyif, k2, yo, [sl1, k2tog, psso, yo, k2tog, yo, k2, B, k1, (k2tog, yo) 2 times, k1, (yo, ssk) 2 times, k1, B, k2, yo, ssk, yo], sl1, k2tog, psso, yo, k3.

Row 21: Sl wyif, k3, [yo, sl1, k2tog, psso, yo, k2, B, k1, k2tog, yo, k2, yo, sl1, k2tog, psso, yo, k2, yo, ssk, k1, B, k2, yo, ssk], yo, ssk, k3.

Row 23: Sl wyif, k2, yo, [sl1, k2tog, psso, yo, k2, B, k1, k2tog, yo, k2, ssk, yo, k1, yo, k2tog, k2, yo, ssk, k1, B, k2, yo], sl1, k2tog, psso, yo, k3.

Row 25: Sl wyif, k3, [k2, yo, ssk, k1, (k2tog, yo) 2 times, k7, (yo, ssk) 2 times, k1, k2tog, yo, k1], k5.

Row 27: Sl wyif, k3, [k3, yo, sl1, k2tog, psso, yo, k2tog, yo, k1, yo, ssk, k3, k2tog, yo, k1, yo, ssk, yo, sl1, k2tog, psso, yo, k2], k5.

Row 29: Sl wyif, k3, [k3, (k2tog, yo) twice, k3, yo, ssk, k1, k2tog, yo, k3, (yo, ssk) 2 times, k2], k5.

Row 31: Sl wyif, k1, k2tog, yo, [k1, yo, ssk, k1, k2tog, yo, k2, B, k2, yo, sl1, k2tog, psso, yo, k2, B, k2, yo, ssk, k1, k2tog, yo], k1, yo, ssk, k2.

Cast On and Garter Stitch Border

Cast on 81 sts.
Rows 1–4: Sl wyif, knit to end.

Work Lace Pattern

Row 1 (RS): Work Row 1 of Lace Pattern chart, working the patt rep 3 times.
Row 2 and all WS rows: Sl wyif, k1, p to last 2 sts, k2.
Continue to work in patt all 48 rows of chart for a total of 8 times.

Garter Stitch Border and Bind-Off

Rows 1–4: Sl wyif, knit to end. Bind off using Russian Bind-Off.

Row 33: Sl wyif, k2, yo, [sl1, k2tog, psso, yo, k1, k2tog, yo, k2, B, k1, k2tog, yo, k1, (yo, ssk) twice, k1, B, k2, yo, ssk, k1, yo], sl1, k2tog, psso, yo, k3.

Row 35: Sl wyif, k1, ssk, yo, [k1, yo, sl1, k2tog, psso, yo, k2, B, k1, (k2tog, yo) 2 times, k1, (yo, ssk) 2 times, k1, B, k2, yo, sl1, k2tog, psso, yo], k1, yo, k2tog, k2.

Row 37: Sl wyif, k3, [k1, k2tog, yo, k2, B, k1, (k2tog, yo) 2 times, k1, (yo, ssk) 3 times, k1, B, k2, yo, ssk], k5.

Row 39: Sl wyif, k2, yo, [sl1, k2tog, psso, yo, k2, B, k1, k2tog, yo, k1, yo, ssk, yo, sl1, k2tog, psso, yo, k2tog, yo, k1, yo, ssk, k1, B, k2, yo], sl1, k2tog, psso, yo, k3.

Row 41: Sl wyif, k3, [k2, yo, ssk, k1, B, k2, (yo, ssk) 2 times, yo, sl1, k2tog, psso, yo, k2tog, yo, k2, B, k1, k2tog, yo, k1], k5.

Row 43: Sl wyif, k1, k2tog, yo, [k1, (yo, ssk) 2 times, k1, B, k2, yo, ssk, yo, sl1, k2tog, psso, yo, k2tog, yo, k2, B, k1, (k2tog, yo) 2 times], k1, yo, ssk, k2.

Row 45: Sl wyif, k2, yo, [sl1, k2tog, psso, yo, k2, yo, ssk, k1, B, k2, yo, ssk, yo, sl1, k2tog, psso, yo, k2, B, k1, k2tog, yo, k2, yo], sl1, k2tog, psso, yo, k3.

Row 47: Sl wyif, k1, ssk, yo, [k1, yo, k2tog, k2, yo, ssk, k1, B, k2, yo, sl1, k2tog, psso, yo, k2, B, k1, k2tog, yo, k2, ssk, yo], k1, yo, k2tog, k2.

Key

	knit		ssk		pattern repeat
O	yo	∧	sl1, k2tog, psso	V	slip purlwise with yarn in front
/	k2tog	B	add bead, then knit		

Lace Pattern

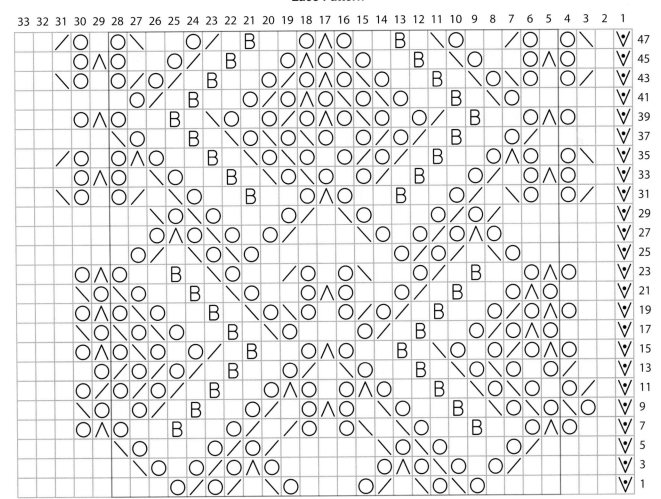

Visual Index

Gillian   28

Eden   33

Alexia   37

Macy   41

Chantelle   46

Lucinda   50

Adelaide   54

Edie   58

Christine   61

Martha   67

Love Hearts   72

Julia   78

Atlantis   81

Leah   88

Ursula   92

Dina   97

Janey   103

Helena   109

Maxine   116   **Catalina   121**   **Ariana   128**

Josephine   133   **Cerina   138**   **Tamar   144**

Chatelaine   148